BUILDING YOUR PERSONAL STOCK PORTFOLIO

BUILDING YOUR PERSONAL STOCK PORTFOLIO

Marian Burk Wood M.B.A

PEARSON

Prentice Hall

Upper Saddle River, New Jersey 07458

Editor-in-Chief: Jeff Shelstad
Senior Editor: Jennifer Simon
Assistant Editor: Ashley Keim
Manager, Print Production: Christy Mahon
Production Editor & Buyer: Carol O'Rourke
Printer/Binder: Courier, Bookmart Press

10 9 8 7 6 5 4
ISBN 0-13-117624-2

TABLE OF CONTENTS

INTRODUCTION TO THE PERSONAL STOCK PORTFOLIO PROJECT

WELCOME TO THE MARKET!

This unique project gives you an opportunity to think and act like an investor. In the coming weeks, you'll learn the basics of investing, from setting an objective and understanding risk to researching and trading stocks. On paper, you (or your team) will have $10,000 to invest in any stocks you choose. At the end of the project, you'll evaluate and discuss the results of your investment decisions.

Of course, investing is much more complex than the basics discussed here. For example, investors need to take into account the tax consequences of their decisions. They also have access to a wider variety of investments and more sophisticated trading choices than in this project.

Please be aware that this book is not intended to provide financial, legal, or other expert advice; recommend any securities; or endorse any resources. If needed, be sure to consult with a professional when you actually begin to invest. The ideas, assignments, and hypothetical examples in this book are designed to help you understand and try investing *on paper only*. The author and publisher are not responsible for any liability, loss, or risk incurred as a consequence, directly or indirectly, of the use and application of any of this book's contents.

PLAN OF THE BOOK

Each chapter in this book introduces some investment concepts, defines key terms, and includes exercises and assignments for individuals or teams. Chapters 1 and 2 (which may be assigned in weeks 1 and 2 of your course) present background about securities, investing, planning, and research. By Chapter 3 (week 3), you'll be selecting your first three stocks. From then on, you'll be tracking your investments and researching additional stocks every week until you reach Chapter 9, unless your instructor gives you different directions. In Chapter 4 (week 4), you'll set up a portfolio tracking system. Chapters 5-10 (weeks 5-10) examine a variety of investment topics. Chapter 11 (week 11) shows how to evaluate performance, and after Chapter 12 (week 12) you present your results.

FEATURES

The chapter-ending activities and assignments will help you explore and apply investment concepts and techniques. "Thinking Critically About Investing" poses thought-provoking questions for individuals or teams to answer. "Using Online Tools to Plan Investments" offers an opportunity to use online resources for investors. Portfolio assignments apply chapter concepts to building a personal stock portfolio. Worksheets guide you through the process of analyzing information, making decisions, and monitoring your paper portfolio.

PORTFOLIO PROJECT RULES

This project can be completed by students working alone or in teams. Most individual investors handle their own research, decisions, and portfolio tracking. However, investment clubs are increasingly popular because they allow the group to benefit from the different skills, knowledge, and perspectives of members.

The portfolio project rules are the same for individuals and teams:

1. You—or your team—will start with $10,000 to invest in common stocks. (In real life, your portfolio would contain a mix of investments.) You will check your portfolio's performance and make trades on Mondays. *(Teams can rotate responsibility for tracking individual stocks but must agree on the investment objective, risk tolerance level, and all trading decisions.)*

2. You must budget a flat commission of $30 for each trade (buy or sell).

3. Buying on a Monday, you will pay the last price reported for each stock at the end of trading on Friday. (If the market was closed on Friday, use the last price reported on Thursday.) When you sell a stock on a Monday, you'll also use the last price from the previous Friday.

4. For your initial portfolio, you must buy at least three different stocks, preferably in different industries. You need not invest the entire $10,000 at once. *(Team members can individually investigate potential investments and report back so the group can make trading decisions.)*

5. Once you've selected your first three stocks, you will fill out the Portfolio Project Tracker forms every week to track your progress. *(Teams can rotate responsibility for entering data but should review the forms before making decisions each week.)*

6. As your instructor directs, be prepared to summarize your investment decisions and results in an oral or written report (weekly or at the close of the project). To supplement your report, you may want to include stock quotation tables or other material related to your stocks or the market. *(Teams can have members work on different parts of the presentation but must agree on the summary of results, decisions, and lessons learned.)*

You (or your team) may want to exchange work with classmates (or other teams), comparing answers to chapter-ending activities, discussing portfolio assignments, and analyzing worksheet entries. Now get ready to build, on paper, your personal stock portfolio.

ABOUT THE AUTHOR

An active investor, Marian Burk Wood has held vice-presidential level positions with Citibank, Chase Manhattan Bank, and the National Retail Federation. With well-known academic experts, she has co-authored undergraduate textbooks on principles of marketing (with Dr. Bill Nickels of University of Maryland), principles of advertising (with Courtland Bovée of Grossmont College), and principles of management (with Courtland Bovée of Grossmont College).

Wood recently authored *The Marketing Plan: A Handbook*, a student guide to developing practical marketing plans. She has also written and edited chapters, cases, features, exercises, print supplements, and electronic supplements, often in collaboration with leading academic authors of business-related college texts. Wood holds an M.B.A. from Long Island University in New York and a B.A. from the City University of New York.

ACKNOWLEDGEMENTS

I want to express my heartfelt appreciation to two talented professionals at Prentice Hall: David Parker, who inspired the idea for this book and shaped its direction; and Ashley Keim, who worked tirelessly on permissions and other key details from start to finish. Thanks also to Morningstar and E*Trade for granting permission to show their Web pages. In addition, I am very grateful to Richard Barnett, Shelley Barnett, and Ray Maki for their insights and comments. Finally, this book is dedicated with love to Heather Werner, Dre Mazzenga, and Katie Goodwin—the next generation of investors.

—Marian Burk Wood, MarianBWW@netscape.net

CHAPTER 1: PLANNING TO INVEST

UNDERSTANDING SECURITIES

If you have any U.S. savings bonds or shares of corporate stock, you own **securities,** investments such as stocks, bonds, and mutual funds. In this personal stock portfolio project, you will be "buying" and "selling" only **common stock,** an investment that gives you an ownership stake in the issuing corporation and a vote in key decisions such as electing the board of directors. Stockholders also receive part of any profits that the corporation decides to distribute in the form of **dividends** (see Chapter 7). In addition, they have the opportunity to make money by selling shares if the stock price rises above the purchase price.

Investors often choose other securities not included in this project, such as:

- **Preferred stock,** which carries a fixed dividend rate but no voting rights. Corporations pay dividends to holders of preferred stock before they pay dividends to holders of common stock, meaning that owners of preferred stock get *preferential* treatment.
- **Bonds,** a corporation's or government entity's legal obligation to repay the amount borrowed (the **face value**) by a certain date (the **maturity**) and to make regular interest payments on that debt. Bond buyers receive a fixed, steady rate of return during the life of the security and receive the face value at maturity.
- **Mutual funds,** which use a pool of investors' money to buy a select group of stocks, bonds, or other securities. This helps you diversify because you own a small piece of all the securities in that fund (see Chapter 10).
- **Futures contracts,** agreements requiring the sale or purchase of a commodity such as corn at a certain price on a specific future date. Because the transaction must be completed even if the commodity's market price on that date is higher or lower than the contract price, investors may lose thousands of dollars on such contracts.

Sometimes a professional is paid to manage the **portfolio**, the group of securities owned by an investor. Some investors hire financial planners to suggest appropriate investment strategies, but not to manage their portfolios. Like many small investors, you will do your own research and make your own investment decisions. Remember that this project does not take into account any tax consequences of investment decisions, however.

MONITORING MARKET INDEXES

During this project, you will be tracking the value of your stock portfolio and evaluating its performance. One measure of a portfolio's success is whether it matches or even beats the performance of the major stock market indexes. The **Dow Jones Industrial Average** (often called the DJIA or simply *the Dow*) follows the stock prices of 30 major U.S. corporations. The **Standard & Poor's 500** (S&P 500) tracks the stock prices of 500 large corporations. The **Russell 2000** is an index covering the stock price of smaller corporations. The **NASDAQ Composite** follows thousands of stocks, mainly younger or high-tech corporations, that are traded *over-the-counter* through the National Association of Securities Dealers network. You can monitor these market indexes by checking online brokerage or news sites (see Appendix 1), major newspapers, and business reports on television or radio.

TRADING COMMON STOCKS

Investors buy and sell common stock (and many other securities) through **brokers,** experts who are licensed to trade securities and receive a **commission** as a fee for their services. Full-service brokerage firms, which provide more personalized service and advice, often set fees according to the number of shares traded or a small percentage of the total trade value. Discount brokerage firms offer less personalized service. These brokers typically charge a flat fee for all trades below a certain level plus a small percentage on larger trades.

Brokers follow the orders you provide. For instance, if you place a **market order**, the broker will act right away, buying or selling at the best price available at that time. If you buy using a **limit order**, the broker will pay no more than the price you specify as the upper limit. If you sell using a limit order, the broker will not sell your stock at less than your specified price. (See Chapter 3 for more about commissions and trading.)

SETTING AN OBJECTIVE

Knowledgeable investing starts with a clear objective. Are you saving for a down-payment on a car or house? Planning to pay for your wedding or a big vacation? Putting money away for a child's college education or for retirement? Think about what you want and estimate the amount of money you'll need. Also think about whether you're investing for the short term (to buy something in a few months) or the long term (to pay for something years from now)?

Depending on your objective, you may buy different securities, buy different amounts of each, and plan your trades differently. As an example, for a long-term investment, you might seek stocks with future growth potential. You might also hold stocks longer to maximize dividend income and allow time for the stockholder equity to grow. For a shorter-term investment, you might buy stock that seems likely to increase in price in the near future. Although securities can fluctuate in value, try to allow enough time to recoup any losses. Rather than seeking one big success, try for a number of small successes that will bring you closer to your objective. In this chapter's assignment, you will choose one specific objective to pursue through your portfolio project.

ASSESSING RISK TOLERANCE

In investing, **risk** refers to the variability of returns. One risk is that share prices or dividend payments will drop when corporations run into problems with money, management, or products. Share prices can fall during a recession, when demand for a corporation's goods or services is lower. Also, inflation may erode the value of a portfolio's return over time—even though the long-term return of common stocks has historically exceeded inflation. And higher interest rates can hurt share prices, as can legal or regulatory actions that hamper corporations.

How much risk can you tolerate? Higher-potential investments tend to be higher risk. You might invest more aggressively for a longer-term objective—if you can tolerate the risk—because you have more time to generate and reinvest returns (and make up for losses). You can use your portfolio to **diversify** with a mix of securities, some riskier and some less risky. For this project, choose stocks unlikely to be affected in the same way by the same risks. All restaurant stocks, for example, are vulnerable to similar risks, so diversify beyond one type of stock.

Now complete the following activities to start your portfolio project.

THINKING CRITICALLY ABOUT INVESTING

1. What are the advantages and disadvantages of a portfolio consisting only of common stock?

   _____

   _____

   _____

   _____

   _____

2. You will be using market indexes to track the market's movement during this project.

   a. Alone or in a team, use library or online sources to identify the 30 stocks in the DJIA:

   _____

   _____

   _____

   _____

   _____

   _____

b. Briefly explain how investors might use the DJIA and the S&P 500 index in planning and managing a personal stock portfolio.

_____

_____

_____

_____

_____

_____

USING ONLINE TOOLS TO PLAN INVESTMENTS

The U.S. Securities and Exchange Commission's EDGAR database contains numerous reports that public corporations must file about their financial situation and future prospects. Go to www.sec.gov/edgar/searchedgar/webusers.htm, click to see the "Quick EDGAR Tutorial," then click on the "Companies & Other Filers" link. Enter the name of a corporation in which you might invest and locate its latest 10-Q quarterly report or 10-K annual report. Look for risks under headings such as "market risk," "factors that may affect future results," and "legal proceedings." ***Save your work on this activity for use in Chapter 2.***

a. What risks are mentioned in this report?

_____

_____

_____

_____

b. Do these risks seem serious enough to deter you from investing in this stock? Why?

_____

_____

_____

_____

c. *Teams:* Locate the 10-Q or 10-K reports of two competing corporations. Compare and contrast the risks listed by the two competitors. Which of the competitors seems like a better short-term investment? Summarize the team's ideas in a brief written or oral report.

PORTFOLIO ASSIGNMENT FOR CHAPTER 1

1. *Set a specific investment objective.*

    a. Identify the specific objective you (or your team) will pursue through the stock portfolio and indicate if it is a long-term or short-term objective.

    _____

    b. Estimate the approximate amount needed to achieve this objective.

    _____

    c. To achieve this objective, when should the money be available?

    _____

2. *Consider your risk tolerance. (Teams: Compare and discuss your answers.)*

    a. Have you ever taken a risk with your money? How did you feel about the outcome?

    _____

    _____

    _____

    b. You just discovered that a toy exactly like one you saved from your childhood is selling for $150 on eBay. Would you sell the toy for the highest price you can get today or would you wait and try to sell it next year, in the hope of getting a higher price? Why?

    _____

    _____

    _____

    c. How would you react if the price of a stock you own fluctuated wildly from day to day?

    _____

    _____

    _____

    d. If you were actually investing money to achieve the objective you set, what would you do if you couldn't generate the needed amount by the deadline?

    _____

    _____

    _____

    _____

e. How upset would you be if the value of an actual investment didn't increase over time?

_____

_____

_____

_____

f. How would you react if you lost some or all of the money you actually invested?

_____

_____

_____

_____

_____

After completing these activities, fill out Worksheet #1.

WORKSHEET #1
OBJECTIVES AND RISK TOLERANCE

Step 1: Summarize your individual or team investment objective in the table below and transfer it to each weekly worksheet to guide your portfolio decisions.

Objective?	Amount needed?	When needed?	Long or short term?

Hint: Although this portfolio project must be completed by the end of the course, you (or your team) can still set a long-term investment objective. One of the criteria for evaluating the portfolio is how well your chosen stocks are faring compared with the overall market and with other stocks in the same industry. Another is the outcome of the trades you make during the project, along with your reasons for buying and selling. Thus, you should not simply set a short-term objective and try to achieve the highest-value portfolio in the class.

Step 2: Understand your risk tolerance. Review your answers to the questions on the previous page, think about your attitudes toward money, and complete the assessment below (alone or as a team). Then write a paragraph about how your risk tolerance (or that of your team) is likely to affect your investment decisions. Remember, this is just a starting point—and there are no right or wrong answers!

- My top priority is to avoid losing any money.   _____ yes _____ no
- I am willing to accept lower return with less risk.   _____ yes _____ no
- I will have little time to make up losses or low returns.   _____ yes _____ no
- I dislike volatility and prefer consistency.   _____ yes _____ no
- My objective is so important that I will minimize risk.   _____ yes _____ no
- I am uncomfortable with great uncertainty.   _____ yes _____ no

                                    Totals: _____ yes _____ no

Scoring: People with more "yes" answers will tend toward a more conservative approach to investing. Those with an equal number of "yes" and "no" answers will seek more diversification and balance in their choices. Those with more "no" answers will feel comfortable with fairly aggressive investment choices.

> **How my risk tolerance is likely to influence my investment decisions:**
>
>
>
>

NAME_____ DATE_____

CHAPTER 2: RESEARCHING STOCK INVESTMENTS

LOCATING COMPANY AND STOCK INFORMATION

In Chapter 1, you set an investment objective and considered your tolerance of risk. Now you're ready to research possible investments. (In real life, you would consider a variety of securities and think about any tax consequences.) Here, the purpose is to identify stocks that might generate the returns needed to meet your objective within the investment period (either short- or long-term)—without more risk than you can tolerate. One place to start is company data.

Public corporations are required to provide annual reports to **stockholders** (also known as **shareholders**), individuals and institutions that own shares of the corporation's stock. In addition, each must submit a **10-K report** to the Securities and Exchange Commission (SEC). The 10-K contains details about corporate finances, operations, risks, and management. The **10-Q report**, submitted every quarter to the SEC, outlines the same information as the 10-K but in less detail.

Brokerage firms and investment research firms offer customers the recommendations of their **securities analysts** (also known as **financial analysts**), specialists who analyze the risks and financial characteristics of securities such as stocks. Analysts' recommendations are also posted on selected Web sites and quoted in news reports. In addition, you can get business and financial news from television, radio, newspapers, business magazines, investor publications such as *Investor's Business Daily* and *Barron's,* and online sources such as CBS MarketWatch.com and the finance area of Yahoo! (see Appendix 1).

RESEARCHING SHARE PRICES

A stock is identified using a combination of letters known as a **stock symbol.** ODP is Office Depot's symbol, for example. You can look up a stock symbol in stock quote tables, on the corporation's Web site, or on financial news sites.

To read a stock quote table, look at the numbered columns in Exhibit A. Remember: stock tables report what happened on the *previous business day.* Column 1 shows the percentage change in share price for the calendar year to date. Columns 2 and 3 show the stock's highest and lowest prices over the past 52 weeks. Columns 4 and 5 show the abbreviated company name and symbol. Column 6 shows the annual cash dividend per share and column 7 shows the dividend yield, the dividend divided by the last share price (see Chapter 7). Column 8 shows the price-earnings ratio, the last share price divided by the annual earnings per share (see Chapter 6). Column 9 shows the number of shares, in hundreds, traded on that day. Column 10 shows the price at which shares ended that day (the **last** or **closing price**). Column 11 shows the net difference between the last price on the day before the reported day and the last price on the reported day. (Sunday's tables show the net change for the week.)

Exhibit A: Reading a Stock Quote Table

❶	❷	❸	❹	❺	❻	❼	❽	❾	❿	⓫
YTD % Chg	52 Weeks High	Low	Stock	Sym	Div	Yld %	PE	Vol 100s	Last	Net Chg
- 1.4	30.68	11.12	Gap Inc	GPS	.09	.7	dd	27593	13.74	-0.20
- 11.5	28	18.35	GardnrDenvr	GDI	...		14	279	19.75	...
- 24.0	13.70	8.20	Gartner	IT	...		dd	2657	8.88	-0.29
- 23.6	13.50	8.05	GartnerB	ITB	...		...	346	8.56	-0.44
- 49.0	16.20	3.80	Gateway	GTW	...		dd	18600	4.10	0.11
- 18.4	29.26	18.49	GaylEnt	GET	...		dd	160	20.08	-1.17
- 15.7	16.25	10.50	GenCorp	GY	.12	1.0	4	1413	11.90	-0.21
- 45.2	58.95	25.10	Genentech	DNA	...		dd	33696	29.75	1.61
- 53.8	19.24	5.59	GenlCbl	BGC	.20	3.3	dd	1699	6.05	-0.20
20.9	111.18	74.90	GenDynam	GD	1.20	1.2	21	28126	96.31	-2.29
- 28.6	47.75	26.40	GenElec	GE	.72	2.5	20	479987	28.60	1.25

Online, you can obtain price quotes by entering a corporation's symbol in the "stock quotation" box of market-related Web sites.

One measure of share price volatility is the stock's **beta.** A beta of 1.0 means the share price tends to increase or decrease in line with the overall market. Stocks with betas higher than 1.0 are more volatile than the overall market, whereas those with betas lower than 1.0 are less volatile. In a **bull market,** where share prices are generally rising, the price of stocks with betas over 1.0 will tend to increase more rapidly than the overall market. In a **bear market,** where share prices are generally dropping, the price of stocks with betas over 1.0 will tend to decrease more rapidly than the overall market. To manage risk, investors try to balance their portfolios with stocks having betas over and under 1.0.

ANALYZING POTENTIAL INVESTMENTS

Before you invest, look at the history of a stock's share price. Where is the current price in relation to the 52-week high and low prices and in between? This is a good starting point, but past trends may not continue, so you need to dig deeper. The more share prices rise above your purchase price, the more money you make.

Because you're becoming a part-owner, you'll want to examine the corporation's current and projected sales and profits. Consider whether experts recommend buying or selling this stock, and what they say about the corporation's profits and stock price. Look up recent news coverage and analyses of the corporation's finances, products, management, legal situation, marketing, and other activities. As you learned in Chapter 1, many factors can affect a stock's current and future risk. For example, the price of General Motors (GM) common stock may fall or stall during an extended recession, because fewer people are buying new cars and sales revenues grow more slowly. Be sure to research the factors that can affect a corporation, its share price, and dividends in the coming months. Also examine the corporation's reputation and its relationships with stakeholders such as employees and community groups, which can affect the stock's performance.

You'll become familiar with additional methods of classifying and analyzing corporate stocks in Chapters 5, 6, and 7. For now, continue your analysis by evaluating the prospects of each potential investment within the context of your objectives, risk tolerance, and investment period.

Complete the following activities to proceed with your portfolio project.

THINKING CRITICALLY ABOUT INVESTING

1. Why should you check the most recent 10-Q report as well as the latest 10-K report when researching a possible stock investment? Why is the use of multiple information sources important for stock research?

_____

_____

_____

_____

2. If you set a long-term objective such as investing for retirement, should you worry about the beta of individual stocks in your portfolio? Explain.

_____

_____

_____

_____

_____

USING ONLINE TOOLS TO PLAN INVESTMENTS

Investment Web sites provide a wealth of in-depth data about corporations, stocks, and industries. To see how one works, visit Quicken at www.Quicken.com and answer these questions about General Electric and two competitors.

a. What is General Electric's stock symbol?

_____

b. What is General Electric's current stock price and 52 week high/low?

_____

a. From the screen showing the full quote, click on the "fundamentals" link and read through the details provided. In terms of growth trends, how does General Electric appear to be doing relative to its industry?

_____

_____

_____

_____

_____

b. *Teams:* Click on the "compare to industry" link and set up a comparison of General Electric with 3M and Siemens, based on "fundamentals." What are the symbols and betas of these three corporate stocks? By beta, which stock most closely tracks the overall market's movement? Which is the least volatile and which the most volatile? Summarize the investment implications in a brief oral or written report.

PORTFOLIO ASSIGNMENT FOR CHAPTER 2

1. *Locate stock symbols and recent stock quotations.* Use your answers to the "Online Tools" activity from Chapter 1 when completing this assignment.

    a. What is the symbol for the corporation in which you might invest?

_____

    b. Using newspaper stock tables or online sources, what are the 52-week high/low share prices and yesterday's last for this corporation's stock?

_____

2. *Look at other factors. (Teams: Compare and discuss your answers.)*

    a. Are the risks you uncovered in this corporation's 10-K or 10-Q report reflected in its recent stock price? In its high/low prices? Explain.

_____

_____

_____

_____

    b. Locate two or three analysts' recommendations and comments about this corporation. What do these analysts say? Have any changed their recommendations lately? Do you agree with their recommendations, based on your 10-Q or 10-K research into this corporation?

_____

_____

_____

_____

_____

c. Search recent news articles for information about this corporation's sales, profits, products, and global business arrangements. What do these reports suggest about the future of the corporation and its stock price?

_____

_____

_____

_____

_____

d. Check the beta of this corporation's stock. How would you expect the share price to behave during a bull market? During a bear market?

_____

_____

_____

_____

e. Read current market reports to find out whether you are likely to be investing in a bull or bear market during this project. What are the implications for this corporation and its stock?

_____

_____

_____

_____

After completing these activities, fill out Worksheet #2.

WORKSHEET #2
RESEARCHING STOCK INVESTMENTS

Step 1: Review the objective that will guide your portfolio decisions.

Objective?	Amount needed?	When needed?	Long or short term?

Step 2: Use your work from the "Online Tools" activities in Chapters 1 and 2 as you answer the following questions about investing in corporate stock.

- I have read the corporation's latest 10-K, 10-Q reports. ____ yes ____ no
- I understand the factors that can affect the stock's risk. ____ yes ____ no
- The potential risks fit with my risk tolerance level. ____ yes ____ no
- Reputable sources see a positive outlook for the stock. ____ yes ____ no
- I understand the beta and the market's current situation. ____ yes ____ no
- Research shows a proven record and promising future. ____ yes ____ no
- The corporation has good stakeholder relations. ____ yes ____ no

Totals: ____ yes ____ no

Scoring: If you have more "yes" than "no" answers, you can make a preliminary decision about becoming a part-owner by buying this corporation's stock. If you have more "no" than "yes" answers, conduct more research to support an informed investment decision about this stock. Research other stocks as well.

Stock:	**Investment decision:**
Why?	
Stock:	**Investment decision:**
Why?	
Stock:	**Investment decision:**
Why?	

NAME_____ DATE_____

CHAPTER 3: BUYING STOCKS FOR YOUR PORTFOLIO

TRADING STOCKS

As you saw in Chapter 1, investors buy and sell stocks through brokers. The first step is to open an account with a brokerage firm and set aside money for buying stocks. Even when you use a full-service broker and receive personalized service and investment advice (in exchange for paying higher commissions), *you* are in charge. A broker may provide research and recommendations, but the decisions and responsibility are ultimately yours.

Whether you deal with your brokerage firm in person, by telephone, or online, you can place orders in several ways. With a market order, you'll get quick action, but you won't know the actual share price until after the trade. You can use a limit order to have your broker buy or sell at a specified price or better. However, as long as the share price remains higher than your buying limit (or lower than your selling limit), the broker won't complete the trade.

In addition, investors can give brokers instructions for specific periods:

- *Day orders.* When you place a **day order**, your instructions apply only for that trading day. At the end of the day, the order automatically expires and you must place a new order if you still want to buy or sell that stock.

- *Open orders.* With an **open order**, your buy or sell instructions stand until the broker executes the trade or until you cancel the order. Your broker may have to wait days or even weeks to execute this trade if the security's price hovers outside the limit you specify.

UNDERSTANDING COMMISSIONS

Once you place an order and the broker executes the trade, your account will be charged a commission for the transaction. How much you pay depends on the type of broker you've chosen and the trading method you use. Many full-service brokerage firms charge more when you talk with your broker in order to complete the transaction. If you enter your orders online, however, brokerage firms generally charge a lower commission, often a flat fee such as $29.95. Discount brokers often charge a flat commission for buying or selling, with a small additional fee tacked on for larger trades.

Suppose you're buying Apple Computer (symbol: AAPL). Based on your research, you decide not to pay more than $22 per share. You go online and place a day order specifying this limit for the purchase of 100 shares. That afternoon, you receive an e-mail message that the brokerage firm executed this trade at $21.75 per share.

What about the commission for this transaction? If the commission is a flat fee of $29.95, your account will be charged that amount when the brokerage firm deducts the cash for your purchase. In this example, the total amount you spent—the amount deducted from your cash—is:

$2,175.00 ($21.75 x 100 shares) + $29.95 = $2,204.95

When you sell, you'll also pay a commission. Assume that you place a market order to sell your 100 shares of Apple, and your broker executes it at a share price of $25. The amount your broker will credit to your account includes what you receive for your shares, minus the amount of the commission:

$2,500.00 ($25.00 x 100 shares) - $29.95 = $2,470.05

In this example, you profited because you sold your stock at a higher share price than the price you paid. Your net profit was $265.10 ($2,470.05 - $2,204.95), taking into account the commissions you paid to buy and sell.

Imagine you decide to sell a stock right away, at a lower price than you paid, because you believe (based on your research) that the price is about to plummet or you want to raise money to invest in a more promising stock. You'll still have to pay a commission when you sell, even if you don't profit from the transaction.

Assume, for instance, that you buy 100 shares of Apple at $25 and sell them at $21.75. At the time of purchase, your account is charged $2,500 ($25 x 100) for the shares and $29.95 for the commission, for a total of $2,529.95. When you sell, your account is credited $2,175 ($21.75 x 100) but the broker deducts $29.95 for the commission, so you receive $2,145.05 after the sale. Including the commissions paid to buy and sell, you lost $384.90.

BUYING STOCKS FOR THIS PROJECT

One of the best ways to learn about investing is to buy and sell on paper, then evaluate the results over time, in the context of your objective and risk tolerance. This simplified portfolio project gives you the opportunity to gain experience in researching and choosing common stocks without risking real cash. (In reality, you would consider the tax consequences and investigate other securities in addition to stocks.) Here are the main rules for this project:

1. You or your team have $10,000 to invest in a portfolio of common stocks. (In real life, your portfolio would be more diversified.) You will check your portfolio's performance and make trading decisions every Monday.

2. You must budget a flat commission of $30 for each trade (buy or sell).

3. Buying on a Monday, you will pay the last price reported for each stock at the close of trading on Friday. (If the market was closed on Friday, use the last price reported on Thursday.) When you sell any stock on a Monday, use the last price from the previous Friday.

4. No market, limit, day, or open orders are allowed in this project. The emphasis is on researching, selecting, and analyzing stocks.

5. For your initial portfolio, you must buy at least three different stocks, preferably in different industries. You need not invest the entire $10,000 at this time. If you want, you may hold some cash for later investments.

STOCK TIPS: USE CAUTION!

In researching stocks, you may come across advice about "hot" stocks. Be wary of stock tips, especially from e-mails, letters, phone calls, or chat rooms. Use caution if you feel pressured to buy a stock that doesn't fit your objective or risk tolerance level. And be on your guard if you see promises of "guaranteed returns" or "double your money." See the SEC site (www.sec.gov) for more cautions.

Remember: No stock can guarantee returns of any kind. In fact, if a corporation in which you invest declares bankruptcy, your shares will usually lose their value. Although stock investments generally have profit potential (especially over long periods), they *always* entail some risk. This project will help you make more informed decisions about investing in stocks. For now, use your research from Chapters 1 and 2 as a starting point for selecting your first three stocks.

Complete the following activities to continue your portfolio project.

THINKING CRITICALLY ABOUT INVESTING

1. Why would an investor place a market order, even though the actual share price won't be known until the trade is executed?

_____

_____

_____

_____

2. How much thought should investors give to the cost of commissions when deciding to buy or sell in the short term? In the long term? Why?

_____

_____

_____

USING ONLINE TOOLS TO PLAN INVESTMENTS

The Motley Fool Web site offers advice and tools for beginners and experienced investors alike. Visit the site (www.fool.com) and browse the latest financial news headlines, look at how the markets are doing, and scan the news and commentary section. Using your work from Chapters 1 and 2, obtain a current quote on this site for one stock in which you might invest. Explore other links on the quote page, including the news, company events, snapshot, research, and messages.

a. What company events are available on this site? Why would such information be valuable to investors? Did you learn anything that affected your view of this stock?

_____

_____

_____

b. What information on this site is particularly useful in evaluating the prospects of the corporation in which you might invest? Did any information cause you to rule out this investment? Explain.

_____

_____

_____

c. *Teams:* Read 10 or more of the messages posted about this corporation. Based on the latest news and stock performance, what do you think about the content of these messages? Do the messages persuade you to buy this stock? Why would people post or read such messages? Summarize the team's findings in a brief oral or written report.

PORTFOLIO ASSIGNMENT FOR CHAPTER 3

1. *Research at least two more stocks for possible purchase.* Apply the information and techniques from earlier chapters as you assess each stock. Consider corporations that you know or that make products you like. Also research corporations that have recently announced acquisitions or mergers.

2. *Select three stocks for your initial portfolio.* On a Monday, make purchase decisions based on your research, objective, and risk tolerance. Follow the rules for stock purchases.

3. *Account for commissions and uninvested cash.* Total your purchases, calculate commissions, and deduct from $10,000. The remainder is uninvested cash.

After completing these activities, fill out Worksheet #3.

WORKSHEET #3
ESTABLISHING YOUR INITIAL PORTFOLIO

Step 1: Review the objective that will guide your portfolio decisions.

Objective?	Amount needed?	When needed?	Long or short term?

Step 2: Research two or more potential stock investments. Document your sources and findings in a separate report, noting: corporation name, symbol, beta, and background (performance, prospects, recommendations, risks, and mergers).

Step 3: Select at least three stocks to purchase on Monday at Friday's last share price (show Friday as the date of buy). Record the details below, using additional sheets for more stocks. Total the amount of your stock holdings. Calculate commissions: ___buys x $30 = $_____. Deduct from $10,000 to arrive at your uninvested cash: $_____. *Save your work for use in Chapter 4.*

Stock name/symbol   Price ($)   # shares   Total ($)   Date of buy

Buy Rationale:

Stock name/symbol   Price ($)   # shares   Total ($)   Date of buy

Buy Rationale:

Stock name/symbol   Price ($)   # shares   Total ($)   Date of buy

Buy Rationale:

NAME_____ DATE_____

CHAPTER 4: TRACKING YOUR PORTFOLIO

PREPARING TO TRACK YOUR SECURITIES

In Chapter 3, you made your first investment decisions. Now it's time to set up a system for monitoring how your stocks fare during the **holding period,** the time during which you own each security. The purpose is to evaluate not only individual stocks but also your portfolio's overall performance. To put your portfolio's performance into context, you will also be tracking changes in major market indexes (DJIA, S&P 500, NASDAQ Composite, and Russell 2000).

You can track your portfolio in several ways:

- *By hand.* Many investors prefer to manually track their portfolios, listing securities and doing all calculations by hand. For this project, you'll use photocopies of the Portfolio Project Tracker forms to track your portfolio by hand every week.

- *With a spreadsheet.* Some investors use a spreadsheet program such as Excel to track their stocks. To do this, you would enter basic information about each stock and then insert formulas for, as an example, calculating the difference between the current price and the purchase of each stock. Then, every time you enter the most current price of that stock, the formula will recalculate the difference. If you know how to use a spreadsheet, you can reduce the time and effort needed to track your portfolio.

- *With personal finance software.* A growing number of investors are using the portfolio tracking capabilities of Quicken, Microsoft Money, or another personal finance program. You enter basic data such as purchase date and share price, and the software handles all the calculations for you. If you have an Internet connection, you can even arrange for the software to automatically update securities prices.

- *On the Web.* You can list your stock purchases and monitor share prices using the free portfolio tracking pages of many finance-oriented Web sites, including Motley Fool, the New York Stock Exchange, and Yahoo! This is a very easy method, and you can even e-mail your portfolio to your instructor or to team members. Exhibit B shows a sample set up on the Web site of online financial services company E*TRADE FINANCIAL.

To start, have all the purchase information from your initial investments handy. Also identify the source you will use to locate updated share prices for each security in your portfolio (review Chapter 2 for sources). In real life, you would search out the most current share price available when tracking your portfolio. For this project, you will update your portfolio and make decisions on Mondays, using the last price at which each of your stocks traded on the Friday before.

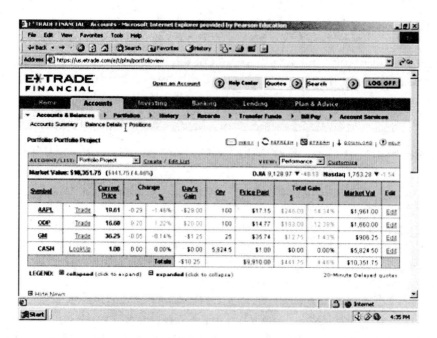

CALCULATING VALUES FOR TRACKING

You've recorded how much you paid for each stock and the date of purchase. For this portfolio project, you'll compare your current **position**—how many shares you own, the current share price, and the resulting value—with your original position (number of shares, purchase price, value). If the net value of your entire portfolio on one Monday is more than it was last Monday, you have a **gain**.

Suppose you purchased two stocks last week: 200 shares at $20 ($4,000) and 100 shares at $40 ($4,000) for a total investment of $8,000. After deducting the commissions for these transactions, you have $1,940 in cash remaining from your original $10,000. Thus, the total value of your portfolio last week was $9,940.

At the end of this week, the last price for the first stock is $25, and the last price for the second stock is $39. Now your positions are worth 200 x $25 ($5,000) and 100 x $39 ($3,900), a total of $8,900. You still have $1,940 in cash, so the current value of your entire portfolio is $10,840, compared with last week's value of $9,940. The difference between this week's value and last week's value is positive. You have a solid gain for the week:

> This week's portfolio value: $10,840
> Last week's portfolio value $ 9,940
> Difference is positive: **gain** $ 900

On the other hand, assume the portfolio value this week is less than it was last week. Then you have a **loss**. Imagine the price of your first stock drops to $18 by the end of this week, and the price of your second stock remains at $40. Now your positions are worth 200 x $18 ($3,600) and 100 x $40 ($4,000) for a total of $7,600. With your $1,940 in cash, the current value of your portfolio is $9,540. The difference between this week's value and last week's value is negative. You have a loss for the week:

> This week's portfolio value: $9,540
> Last week's portfolio value $9,940
> Difference is negative: **loss** $ 400

Clearly, every investor wants to achieve gains over time, even if individual stocks (or the entire portfolio) periodically show losses. When you're investing for the long term—such as for retirement—you have a much better chance of being able to recoup losses by the time you need the money. Even if your objective is short-term, it's possible to end with a gain if you do your homework before buying securities, diversify your holdings, track your portfolio, and do your homework to make timely, informed decisions about buying, holding, and selling.

COMPARING YOUR PORTFOLIO WITH THE MARKET

Another measure of investment progress is to compare your portfolio's movement with the overall market's movement. This is where the market indexes come into play. To get a good overview of the market's movement, you'll track the DJIA, S&P 500, NASDAQ Composite, and Russell 2000 indexes at the start of each week (using the Friday closing level, found in Sunday newspapers and financial Web sites) and compare their direction with the direction of your portfolio. In addition, you can compare stocks in certain industries with specialized indexes; if you buy an airline or a railroad stock, you could measure its progress against the Dow Jones Transportation Average.

If your stocks show a significant loss while the indexes show significant gains, take a closer look at your investments. Use your weekly research to find out why your stocks are not doing as well as the market. If the indexes rise and your investments do not, you may want to consider selling some stocks and buy others after checking out the corporations and their management. If your portfolio outperforms the market, congratulations—for now. Remember, good returns in the past are no guarantee of good returns in the future. The one constant in the market is constant change, so do your homework and be prepared.

Complete the following activities to continue your portfolio project.

THINKING CRITICALLY ABOUT INVESTING

1. Why is it helpful to look at the weekly percentage change in market indexes when assessing the performance of each stock and your overall portfolio?

_____

_____

_____

_____

2. How can researching a corporation's management and quality help you understand the stock's past performance and potential for the future?

_____

_____

_____

_____

USING ONLINE TOOLS TO PLAN INVESTMENTS

The CNN Money site is a good gateway to market news and analyses. On the home page at http://money.cnn.com, note which indexes are tracked and the current direction of each. You can locate stock symbols, get quotes, and check business headlines here. Follow the "markets and stocks" link for more details about the indexes and for market commentary. Then move to the "Dow 30" link and explore that page.

a. Why would investors value graphical depictions of each index's daily ups and downs?

_____

_____

_____

_____

b. What information is available on the "Dow 30" page? What information from this page might be useful to you as an investor?

_____

_____

_____

_____

_____

c. *Teams:* Read a few of the headlines and the market commentary on the "markets and stocks" page. How does the commentary explain the market patterns you see in the graphs and statistics on this site? What effect do the news reports appear to be having on the market indexes? What are the implications for individual stocks in your portfolio? Summarize your team's findings in a brief oral or written report.

PORTFOLIO ASSIGNMENT FOR CHAPTER 4

1. *Research the latest news about each stock you own.* Each Monday, using the online tools and portfolio assignments from this and earlier chapters, find out what happened to the corporation, its management, and its stock in the past week. If any of your stocks declared or paid dividends during the week, note the amount separately (this will be discussed in more detail in Chapter 7).

2. *Assess stock and market performance.* Look up Friday's last price for each stock (the "current price") and calculate the current value of your positions, stock by stock. Summarize the corporation's situation and think about how recent developments have affected or are likely to affect the share price. Also note the current value (based on the Friday's closing value) of the major market indexes.

3. *Decide whether to hold or sell each stock.* Review your research, objective, and risk tolerance as you decide whether to hold or sell each stock. Remember that you <u>must</u> sell at least one stock and buy another during this project. For peer review, discuss your research and decisions with a classmate.

4. *Research at least one more stock for potential purchase.* Even if you've invested the entire $10,000, research at least one more stock that you would consider purchasing in the future. Examine the management and the quality, and be prepared to champion the purchase of this stock to your team or to the class. If you have enough uninvested cash, you can buy more shares of a stock you already hold or buy shares of another stock, following the rules for purchases.

5. *Decide on trades, then calculate commissions and your total portfolio value.* Once you've decided on any trades, add up the number of buy and sell transactions and multiply by $30. Deduct this amount to determine your current total portfolio value for this week. Then calculate the difference in your portfolio's value between the current week and the previous week.

Now photocopy and complete the Portfolio Project Tracker forms, following the directions on Worksheet #4.

WORKSHEET #4
TRACKING YOUR PORTFOLIO

Step 1: Review the objective that will guide your portfolio decisions.

Objective?	Amount needed?	When needed?	Long or short term?

Step 2: Working on a photocopy of Portfolio Project Tracker Part 1, enter the purchase price and the current price of each stock you own in Part 1A. Calculate the original value of your positions (purchase price x number of shares) and the current value of your positions (current price x number of shares). Deduct the current value from the purchase value to determine gain/loss per stock. Note any uninvested cash (after deducting commissions, see Worksheet #3).

Step 3: Summarize this week's research about each stock, including corporate management, on a photocopy of the Portfolio Project Tracker Part 2.

Step 4: On Monday, if you decide to sell stock(s) based on this week's research, use Friday's last share price. Record the trade details in Part 1B but wait to record commissions until Step 6.

Step 4: If you are buying additional stocks, research new stocks in Part 2A and document your trades (using Friday's last share price) in Part 1B. List each stock trade on a separate line and hold commissions until Step 6.

Step 5: Fill out Part 1C to show your positions after this week's trades. Adjust the uninvested cash to reflect your trades. Now add all current positions to arrive at your total portfolio holdings, and transfer this figure to Part 2B.

Step 6: In Part 2B, calculate this week's commissions by multiplying the number of buy or sell trades by $30. Deduct the commissions to calculate your current total portfolio value for the week. Compare this with the value of last week's portfolio and note the difference in dollars. Also indicate whether your portfolio shows an overall gain or loss.

Step 7: List the current value (Friday's closing value) of the four market indexes in Part 1B. For this week __only__, do not show any "last week's value" for these indexes. Starting next week, you'll be comparing the current and previous week's values for all four indexes.

Hint: To get ready for next week, make new photocopies of the Portfolio Project Tracker forms. Enter the data from this week's Part 1C in Part 1A of next week's form and enter this week's market index figures on Part 2C of next week's form. You'll be following the same procedure every week during this project.

NAME_____ DATE_____

CHAPTER 5: CLASSIFYING STOCKS

UNDERSTANDING STOCK CLASSIFICATIONS

In assembling a portfolio to meet your objective within your risk tolerance, you can choose from thousands of corporate stocks. (Remember, your real-life portfolio would include other securities in addition to stocks, for diversification.) Investment experts classify stocks in a variety of ways:

- *By capitalization.* **Large-cap stocks** (short for **large-capitalization**) are stocks of major corporations that have issued millions of shares and have a high total market value (*capitalization*). **Small-cap stocks** are corporations with a much smaller market value, and **mid-cap stocks** are those with a medium market value. Most corporations with household names, such as Walt Disney (DIS) and Hewlett-Packard (HPQ), are large-cap stocks. Because large-cap stocks are well known and widely owned, you can easily research their prospects and buy or sell your stake.

  If you're interested in a small-cap stock, you may have more difficulty researching it, buying, and selling. This is because relatively few shares trade each day (compared with the huge trading volumes of large-cap stocks), and the smallest firms don't have to file SEC reports. Smaller corporations are younger and have less capital but some are more innovative than giant competitors. So if a small-cap stock scores a big success, your shares could soar in value. Carefully assess the potential risks and rewards before you buy.

- *By objective.* For short-term investments, consider **income stocks**, which pay relatively high dividends every quarter. Utilities are a good example. Despite the dividends, don't expect the kind of dramatic price increases (or decreases) you might get with small-cap stocks, for example. For long-term investments, look at **growth stocks**, which have a record of growth and are expected to continue growing steadily, yielding good investor returns in the future. Depending on your objective, consider **value stocks**, which appear to be priced low at the moment relative to their earnings and future potential.

- *By economic cycle.* The financial performance of certain corporations are influenced by the economic cycle. **Cyclical stocks** are stocks of corporations more closely tied to the direction of the economy, such as car manufacturers. Such stocks tend to do well in good economic periods but not as well in recessions. In contrast, **counter-cyclical stocks** are stocks of corporations with performances that run in the opposite direction from the economy. These stocks tend to do well when the economy is faltering but not as well when the economy is expanding. **Defensive stocks** are less closely tied to economic cycles and market swings; these generally have betas below 1.

- *By record.* **Blue-chip stocks** are large-cap stocks that have a long history of profits and dividends, such as Johnson & Johnson (JNJ). Although these stocks are considered among the highest-quality stock investments, remember that past performance is no guarantee of future performance. At some point, these corporations may suffer poor sales and profits or lower their dividend payments.

Many stocks fit into more than one classification. A cyclical stock may also be an income stock and a large-cap stock, for example. Securities analysts and market watchers sometimes disagree on how a particular stock should be classified (other than size). One expert's growth stock may be another expert's value stock.

Moreover, corporate decisions, economic circumstances, and other factors can change a stock's classification. When McDonald's (MCD) was opening outlets around the world and expanding rapidly, it was considered a growth stock. When its global expansion finally slowed and profits faltered, many investors sold their shares. That drove the share price down—making the company seem like a value stock to investors who believed the fast-food giant would return to high-profit performance in the near future.

USING CLASSIFICATION IN PORTFOLIO DECISIONS

Why should you care how a stock is classified? Because the market is filled with investment choices, classifying stocks helps you put together a portfolio with some diversification. If your entire portfolio consisted of cyclical stocks, for example, the value would be more prone to stall or fall during an economic downturn. Similarly, if you invested only in blue-chip stocks, you would miss the opportunity for possible future gains from growth stocks.

Understanding how stocks are classified also helps you tailor your portfolio to your objective and your risk tolerance. For instance, if you are conservative and want to minimize risk, you might think about including blue-chip stocks. If your objective is to make money in the short term, or if you want to generate a steady income over a particular period, you'll think about including income stocks. If you have an ambitious investment objective, you might consider a mix of small-cap stocks (for possibly higher returns) and large-cap stocks (for more stability). Your exact choices depend on your individual situation and the results of your research and analyses.

Some publications and Web sites help you screen stocks according to classification and other specifications. Using Morningstar.com, for example, you can screen stocks and mutual funds according to industry (sector), stock type (such as cyclical), market capitalization, and other criteria. Exhibit C shows the stock screener at this site.

Now complete the chapter-ending activities to continue your portfolio project.

Exhibit C: Morningstar's Stock Screener

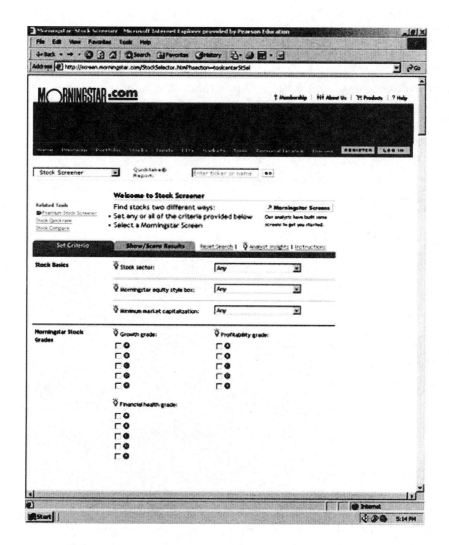

THINKING CRITICALLY ABOUT INVESTING

1. What are the advantages and disadvantages of investing in large-cap stocks? In small-cap stocks?

_____

_____

_____

_____

2. Should you reexamine the classification of stocks you own as well as researching the classification of stocks you're considering for purchase?

_____

_____

_____

USING ONLINE TOOLS TO PLAN INVESTMENTS

Every month, *Smart Money* magazine analyzes a particular industry or type of stock for investors to consider. If you had taken the magazine's advice about a stock, how would you have fared? The magazine shows you on its Web site at http://www.smartmoney.com/magportfolios. Click on one of the recent articles about stocks, note the original date, and read the reasoning behind the magazine's picks. Then scroll down to the bottom and check the share price for each featured stock when the article was written and the share price today.

a. Why did *Smart Money* originally recommend these stocks? How would you classify these stocks? How are the stocks doing now?

_____

_____

_____

_____

b. What are the advantages and disadvantages of using recommendations from *Smart Money* and other financial publications when selecting stocks?

_____

_____

_____

_____

c. *Teams:* Pick one of the featured stocks and use the *Smart Money* Web site to find out more about the corporation, its market capitalization, and its competition (start with the stock quote function). Also check how analysts are rating this stock. Finally, visit the company's Web site and read about its products and performance. Based on this research, would you consider buying this stock today? Summarize the team's ideas in a brief oral or written report.

PORTFOLIO ASSIGNMENT FOR CHAPTER 5

1. *Determine how your stocks can be classified.* Which of your stocks are large-cap, which are blue-chip, which are growth stocks, and so on? Does your portfolio contain mostly stocks of one classification?

2. *Research the latest news about each stock you own.* Find out what happened to the corporation and its stock in the past week. If any of your stocks declared

or paid dividends during the week, note the amount separately (this will be discussed in more detail in Chapter 7).

3. *Assess stock and market performance.* Look up the previous Friday's last price and calculate the value of each stock you hold. Summarize the corporation's situation and discuss how recent developments have affected or may affect the share price. Also note the current value (based on the previous Friday's closing value) of the major market indexes.

4. *Decide whether to hold or sell each stock.* Review your research, objective, and risk tolerance as you decide whether to hold or sell each stock. Look at overall market trends and review the reason you originally bought each stock. Think about the consequences of holding or selling each stock. Are the corporation's profits still on track? Has corporate growth or profitability peaked? Is the industry starting to decline? Has the share price skyrocketed, offering you the opportunity to "lock in" gains by selling while the share price is high? (You <u>must</u> sell at least one stock and buy another during this project.) Discuss your decisions with a classmate or team members for peer review.

5. *Research at least one more stock for potential purchase, and decide on trades.* Research at least one more stock (perhaps from a different industry or a corporation that is familiar) that you would consider purchasing in the future. Be prepared to discuss its classification and how that classification fits with the stocks you already own. If you have uninvested cash, you can buy shares of this stock, another stock, or additional shares of a stock you already hold, following the rules for purchases on Mondays.

6. *Calculate commissions and your total portfolio value.* Once you've decided on any trades, add up the number of buy and sell transactions and multiply by $30. Deduct this amount to determine your current total portfolio value for this week. Finally, calculate the portfolio value change from the previous week.

After completing these activities, continue to Worksheet #5. If you haven't already done so, photocopy the Portfolio Project Tracker forms for this week.

WORKSHEET #5
CLASSIFYING STOCKS

Step 1: Review the objective that will guide your portfolio decisions.

Objective?	Amount needed?	When needed?	Long or short term?

Step 2: Indicate below how each stock you hold can be classified. Briefly explain the implications for your portfolio in Part 2A of the Portfolio Project Tracker form. Given the classification of your stocks, would you make different investment decisions?

Stock   Classification

_____

_____

_____

_____

Step 3: Copy the portfolio information from Part 1C on last week's Portfolio Project Tracker form to Part 1A on this week's form.

Step 4: Summarize this week's stock research and decisions in Part 2A.

Step 5: If you decide to sell anything on Monday based on this week's research or your classification of the stock, use Friday's last share price. Record the trade details in Part 1B but wait to record commissions until Step 7. If you buy any stocks, summarize your research in Part 2A and indicate how the stock(s) can be classified. Document your trades using Friday's last share price in Part 1B but hold commissions until Step 7.

Step 6: Fill out Part 1C to show your positions after this week's trades. Adjust the uninvested cash to reflect your trades. Now add all current positions to arrive at your total portfolio holdings, and transfer this figure to Part 2B.

Step 7: In Part 2B, calculate this week's commissions by multiplying the number of buy or sell trades by $30. Deduct the commissions to calculate your current total portfolio value for the week. Compare this with the value of last week's portfolio and note the difference in dollars. Also indicate whether your portfolio shows an overall gain or loss.

Step 8: List the current value (Friday's closing value) of the four market indexes in Part 2C. Note whether the indexes are moving higher or lower and compare their movement with the change (gain or loss) in your portfolio's value.

NAME_____ DATE_____

CHAPTER 6: ANALYZING PERFORMANCE TRENDS

EXAMINING REVENUE AND EARNINGS TRENDS

Investors should examine certain basic performance trends before buying a corporation's stock. Start with the sales revenue and earnings figures for this year and previous years. The annual report, the 10K, and often the corporate Web site can provide this information so you can analyze the historical trends. Ideally, you're looking for a corporation with a record of steadily rising revenue and earnings—especially one with better trends than the industry. When a poor economy or other factors are dampening revenue and earnings growth, you may want to look for corporations that are at least outperforming their competitors.

Remember, by investing, you're becoming a part-owner in these corporations. Unless your research convinces you that a major turnaround or sales breakthrough is imminent, why would you want to own part of a corporation that lags far behind its industry or reports ever-lower revenue and earnings?

Another way to look at earnings is to note the **earnings per share (EPS)**, which is calculated by dividing reported net earnings by the total number of common stock shares outstanding. The EPS shows you how much in earnings the corporation generates for a single share of stock. For example, if Kellogg (K) reported net earnings of $732 million and had 400 million outstanding shares, its EPS would be $1.83, calculated this way:

$$\frac{\$732,000,000}{400,000,000} = \$1.83$$

Imagine that through research, you learn that Kellogg's EPS for the last fiscal year was $1.80 and its EPS for the fiscal year before was $1.75. In this example, the three-year EPS trend is moving steadily upward—a good sign.

Historical trends are no guarantee of future performance, but you can get some idea of how a company has been doing through such analyses. To be as up-to-date as possible, you may want to do what many analysts do: Use the corporation's projected earnings for the upcoming fiscal year—rather than earnings figures from the last 12 months—when calculating EPS.

UNDERSTANDING PRICE-EARNINGS ANALYSIS

Once you know the EPS, you can calculate the **price-earnings (P/E) ratio** by dividing the corporation's stock price by its reported EPS for the year. Assume that Kellogg's share price is $35 and its EPS is $1.80. The P/E ratio would be 35/1.80 = 19.44. No need to calculate this on your own; you can find EPS figures in the stock tables and online (see Exhibit A in Chapter 2). Note that a company without profits will have no p/e shown in the table.

Analysts often calculate a forward P/E ratio by projecting the corporation's future earnings rather than using its historical earnings. Using even more sophisticated analyses, they also examine the P/E in relation to future EPS growth and other growth measures. Healthy earnings growth attracts additional investors, which pushes the share price higher, a positive development if you buy at a lower price and sell at a higher price. Therefore, when you look at a stock's P/E, examine the corporation's prospects for growth as well as its previous earnings.

Also, compare a corporation's P/E with the P/E of the overall market and the P/E of others in the same industry. If the corporation's P/E is much lower than the market and its competitors, the corporation is either having difficulty or is an undiscovered value stock—a potential bargain if earnings go up. If the corporation's P/E is much higher than the industry and the market, the stock could well be overvalued and not as attractive to purchase at this point.

Yet a corporation with a P/E higher than its industry may not be overvalued if it is in a period of rapid growth, especially growth far in excess of its competitors. Because so many factors can affect a stock's valuation, however, never base your trading decisions solely on your P/E analysis.

RESEARCHING HISTORICAL SHARE PRICES

Although no one can pinpoint the best time to buy or sell a stock, understanding share price trends can help in your decision. In Chapter 2, you learned about 52-week high/low share prices. Stocks at or near their 52-week highs may seem overvalued and could go lower, whereas those at or near 52-week lows may seem undervalued and could go higher. Still, you might buy a stock near its 52-week high because research suggests even more growth ahead. Or you might avoid a stock near its 52-week low because research suggests problems ahead.

Share prices are constantly changing, so look at the pattern of price changes during a recent trading day *(intraday)* as well as making day-to-day, week-to-week, and month-to-month comparisons of closing prices. Charts are an excellent way to depict such patterns. Many publications and Web sites feature charts showing the movement of stocks and major market indexes during the previous trading day and, in some cases, for the past 12 months. Think about short-term and long-term share price volatility and check the beta as you examine these charts and consider the potential risk.

See if the price is moving generally upward or downward over a period of months, and compare the trend with that of the overall market. Is the price moving upward toward the 52-week high level? Or is it moving downward toward the 52-week low level? Did a new product introduction, special promotion, or other event cause the peaks and valleys—and is the corporation likely to go through something similar in the future? These are only some of the issues you can explore as you research historical share prices.

GOING BEYOND THE NUMBERS

Analysts and sophisticated investors use even more technical methods of examining a stock's financials. However, they also look beyond P/E figures and share price trends when considering whether to buy, hold, or sell. Follow their lead and carefully research each corporation's overall finances, products, operations, management, labor relations, marketing, risks, legal situation, industry, and plans. Also consider analysts' recommendations, recent upgrades or downgrades, and economic conditions. These are some of the many factors—including the movement of the overall market—that can affect share price.

Now complete the chapter-ending activities to continue your portfolio project.

THINKING CRITICALLY ABOUT INVESTING

1. As an investor, what kind of difference would you hope to see if you calculated one of your stock's P/E with previously reported earnings and then calculated the P/E with projected future earnings?

_____

_____

_____

_____

_____

2. Why would you look at a chart of a stock's 1-year price pattern in addition to checking its 52-week high-low prices in a stock table?

_____

_____

_____

_____

USING ONLINE TOOLS TO PLAN INVESTMENTS

Different Web sites display EPS, P/E, and historical share price trends in different ways. For this exercise, visit www.dailystocks.com. Browse the home page, which is loaded with links to other investment-related sites. In the box for stock symbols (called "tickers" here), enter SBUX to look at data for Starbucks. If you prefer, you can enter the symbol of a stock in your portfolio.

a. What is the current P/E of this stock?

_____

b. What is the trend in quarterly EPS for this stock?

_____

c. Now switch to the chart view for this stock. What is the share price trend for the most recent month? For the past 3 months? For the past 6 months?

_____

_____

_____

_____

_____

d. *Teams:* Using what you learned about the EPS trend, share price trend, and P/E, what is your impression of how the market is valuing this stock? What other information on this site could help you better understand this stock? Summarize the team's comments in a brief oral or written report.

PORTFOLIO ASSIGNMENT FOR CHAPTER 6

1. *Look up the P/E, EPS, and historical price trends for each stock you own.* What patterns do you see in the historical price trends? How do the trends of your stocks compare with overall market trends? What can you find out about the P/E and EPS of competitors in the same industry as the corporations in which you own shares? Looking at your earlier research, what are the growth prospects for each stock you own?

2. *Research the latest news about each stock you own.* Find out what happened to the corporation and its stock in the past week. Is it expanding or reducing its workforce? If some of its employees are unionized, does the corporation have good relations with organized labor? If your stock declared or paid dividends during the week, note the amount separately (see more detail in Chapter 7).

3. *Assess stock and market performance.* Look up the previous Friday's last price and calculate the current value of your positions. Summarize the corporation's situation and discuss how recent developments affected or may affect the share price. Also note the current value (based on the previous Friday's closing value) of the major market indexes.

4. *Decide whether to hold or sell each stock.* Review your research, objective, and risk tolerance as you decide whether to hold or sell each stock. Remember that you <u>must</u> sell at least one stock and buy another during this project. If you do so on Monday of this week, discuss your decisions and reasoning with a classmate or your team members.

5. *Research at least one more stock for potential purchase.* Research at least one additional stock that you would consider purchasing in the future. As you examine the corporation, look at its management, its labor situation, and how employees are motivated. Also be prepared to discuss its EPS and P/E ratio. If you buy this or another stock, follow the rules for purchase.

6. *Calculate commissions and your total portfolio value.* Once you've decided on any trades, add up the number of buy and sell transactions and multiply by $30. Deduct this amount from the current value of your holdings to determine your total portfolio value for this week. Finally, calculate the portfolio value change from the previous week.

After completing these activities, fill out Worksheet #6. Use fresh photocopies of the Portfolio Project Tracker forms for this week.

WORKSHEET #6
ANALYZING TRENDS

Step 1: Review the objective that will guide your portfolio decisions.

Objective?	Amount needed?	When needed?	Long or short term?

Step 2: Record below the EPS and P/E of each stock you hold. What do you think of the P/E ratios for each stock? Given what you now know about EPS and P/E, would you make different investment decisions? Briefly explain the implications for your stocks in Part 2A of the Portfolio Project Tracker form.

Stock   EPS   P/E

_____

_____

_____

_____

Step 3: Copy the portfolio information from Part 1C on last week's Portfolio Project Tracker form to Part 1A on this week's form.

Step 4: Summarize this week's stock research and decisions in Part 2A.

Step 5: If you decide to sell anything based on this week's research, your knowledge of its human resources management, or EPS and P/E, use Friday's last share price. Record the trade details in Part 1B (hold commissions for Step 7). If you are buying any stocks, summarize your research in Part 2A. Document your trades using Friday's last share price in Part 1B (hold commissions for Step 7).

Step 6: Fill out Part 1C to show your positions after this week's trades. Adjust the uninvested cash to reflect your trades. Now add all current positions to arrive at your total portfolio holdings, and transfer this figure to Part 2B.

Step 7: In Part 2B, calculate this week's commissions by multiplying the number of buy or sell trades by $30. Deduct the commissions to calculate your current total portfolio value for the week. Compare this with the value of last week's portfolio and note the difference in dollars. Also indicate whether your portfolio shows an overall gain or loss.

Step 8: List the current value (Friday's closing value) of the four market indexes in Part 2C. Note whether the indexes are moving higher or lower and compare their movement with the change in your portfolio's value.

NAME_____ DATE_____

CHAPTER 7: UNDERSTANDING DIVIDENDS

INVESTING WITH DIVIDENDS IN MIND

Many public corporations distribute part of their profits to stockholders in the form of dividends. Such distributions can take several forms, including:

- *Cash dividend.* Most of the time, established corporations pay quarterly cash dividends. Every shareholder is entitled to receive the dividend (a few cents or even a few dollars per share) in cash or—at the shareholder's option—can reinvest the dividend to buy more shares. Blue-chip stocks are considered less risky because of a long history of paying regular cash dividends. You can look up annual dividends in stock quote tables (see Exhibit A in Chapter 2).

- *Stock dividend.* Sometimes corporations conserve cash by distributing dividends in the form of stock, known as a **stock dividend**. This increases the **shares outstanding**—the number of shares that have been issued and are owned by investors (not by the corporation). In turn, the EPS goes down because earnings are spread across more shares. Stock dividends are indicated by the notation "t" or "stk" in the dividend column of stock tables.

- *Share buyback.* When corporations use **share buyback plans** (also known as **stock repurchase plans** or simply **buybacks**), they are offering to buy shares back from stockholders at a specific price exceeding the market price at that time. Stockholders are not required to sell any or all their shares back, but those who do will receive cash. A buyback reduces the number of shares outstanding and increases the EPS now that earnings are spread across fewer shares. If this makes the stock seem more attractive to new investors and drives the price up, stockholders will benefit.

As you can see by checking the stock quote tables, not all corporations pay dividends. Some conserve cash for new products and other internal needs. Corporations that pay quarterly dividends declare (announce) the amount in advance and state that stockholders as of a certain date will receive the payment.

CALCULATING DIVIDEND YIELD

Investors are always interested in returns. You can calculate the return generated by a stock's dividend by dividing the annual dividend by the current share price, giving you the **dividend yield**. Assume that the annual dividend of Wells Fargo Bank (WFC) is $1.20 and its share price is $50. The dividend yield would be:

$$\frac{1.20}{50.00} = .024 \text{ or } 2.4\%$$

In this example, the $1.20 dividend equals 2.4% of Wells Fargo's current share price. A quick way to find out a corporation's dividend yield is to check the stock quote tables; note that the dividend yield will change as share prices change.

TAKING DIVIDENDS INTO ACCOUNT

Why is the dividend yield important? A lower yield means you will be getting a smaller return in relation to the share price; a higher yield means you will be getting a larger return in relation to share price. So, if receiving quarterly dividend payments will help you reach your investment objective, look at the dividend yield when researching stocks. If you believe that a corporation's share price will move higher in the future, you can arrange to automatically reinvest dividends by buying additional shares in that corporation. Another option is to have cash dividends paid into your brokerage account so you can buy other securities.

Note that some corporations choose to pay no dividends because they use profits for new products and other expansion-related needs. These corporations may be growing more aggressively than corporations paying dividends, and if they have solid earnings growth, the stock seems more attractive to new investors. This drives the share price higher. As a result, investors who bought the stock earlier will benefit from the **appreciation** when the price of their shares goes up.

If the share price of a dividend-paying corporation drops, the dividend yield will be even higher; if the share price rises, the dividend yield will be lower. Although the dividend amount can vary, corporations with a long history of dividends—such as the blue-chips—rarely stop paying unless they're in serious difficulty, and they may even raise dividends at certain points. If you hold such stocks for long periods or if you have large holdings, the total dividends can be substantial.

NOTE: When you invest on your own, you'll need to review the tax implications of dividends and share price appreciation, which are not part of this project.

Complete these chapter-ending activities to continue your portfolio project.

THINKING CRITICALLY ABOUT INVESTING

1. Under what circumstances might you have cash dividends paid into your account rather than reinvesting in more shares?

_____

_____

_____

_____

_____

2. What should an investor consider when deciding whether to sell shares to the corporation during a buyback?

_____

_____

_____

_____

_____

USING ONLINE TOOLS TO PLAN INVESTMENTS

A number of financial Web sites can help you research stocks according to dividend yield and other criteria. Browse MSN Money Central's home page at http://moneycentral.msn.com. Next, follow the link to "investing" and select "stock screener." On that page, set two criteria: (1) membership in the Dow Jones Industrial Average and (2) dividend yield "as high as possible." Then click on search to see which stocks in the Dow have the highest dividend yield.

a. What is the highest dividend yield among the Dow stocks shown in the stock screener's results? What is the lowest current dividend yield?

_____

_____

b. Now return to the stock screener page and set the dividend yield to "as low as possible." What is the lowest dividend yield among these results? The highest dividend yield? What type of corporations have the highest dividend yield in the Dow? What type have the lowest dividend yield?

_____

_____

_____

c. *Teams:* Click on the symbol of one stock in the high-dividend-yield list. Read its profile and examine share price trends, beta, EPS trends and forecasts, financials, analyst consensus, and other details on this page. Would you recommend buying this stock? Summarize the team's conclusion and rationale in a brief report.

PORTFOLIO ASSIGNMENT FOR CHAPTER 7

1. *Find out whether your stocks pay dividends.* Use online research and earlier portfolio assignments to determine whether a corporation in which you have invested either declared or paid a dividend while you held its stock. Continue to note any dividends that are declared or paid until the end of the project. You will be including dividend income when you calculate the final value of your portfolio (see Chapter 11). For now, look at the recent trend in quarterly dividend payments and the dividend yield for each of your stocks. Would you change any of your previous buy and sell decisions now that you know more about dividends? Prepare a brief oral or written explanation.

2. *Research the latest news about each stock you own.* Find out what happened to the corporation and its stock in the past week. If one of your stocks declared or paid dividends during the week, note the amount separately.

3. *Assess stock and market performance.* Look up the previous Friday's last price and calculate the current value of your positions. Summarize each corporation's situation and discuss how recent developments affected or may affect the share price. Also note the current value (based on the previous Friday's closing value) of the major market indexes.

4. *Decide whether to hold or sell each stock.* Review your research, objective, and risk tolerance as you decide whether to hold or sell each stock on a Monday. You <u>must</u> sell at least one stock and buy another during this project. If you do so this week, discuss your decisions and reasoning with a classmate or your team members.

5. *Research at least one more stock for potential purchase.* Research at least one additional stock that you would consider purchasing in the future. Be prepared to discuss its dividend policy, recent dividend payments (if any), and dividend yield. If you buy this or another stock, follow the rules for purchase.

6. *Calculate commissions and your total portfolio value.* Once you've decided on any trades, add up the number of buy and sell transactions and multiply by $30. Deduct this amount from the current value of your holdings to determine your total portfolio value for this week. Finally, calculate the portfolio value change from the previous week.

After completing these activities, fill out Worksheet #7, using fresh photocopies of the Portfolio Project Tracker forms.

WORKSHEET #7
UNDERSTANDING DIVIDENDS

Step 1: Review the objective that will guide your portfolio decisions.

Objective?	Amount needed?	When needed?	Long or short term?

Step 2: Note below the dividend policy, annual dividend, and dividend yield of each stock you own (as of Friday). Given your objective, would you change any of the trading decisions you made now that you know more about dividends? Include your comments in Part 2A of the Portfolio Project Tracker form.

Stock   pays dividends?   annual dividend   dividend yield

_____

_____

_____

_____

_____

Step 3: Copy the portfolio information from Part 1C on last week's Portfolio Project Tracker form to Part 1A on this week's form.

Step 4: Summarize this week's stock research and decisions in Part 2A.

Step 5: If you decide to sell anything based on this week's research or dividend data, use Friday's last share price. Record the trade in Part 1B but wait to record commissions until Step 7. If you are buying any stocks, summarize your research and their dividend situations in Part 2A. Document your trades using Friday's last share price in Part 1B (hold commissions for Step 7).

Step 6: Fill out Part 1C to show your positions after this week's trades. Adjust the uninvested cash to reflect your trades. Now add all current holdings to arrive at your total portfolio holdings, and transfer this figure to Part 2B.

Step 7: In Part 2B, calculate this week's commissions by multiplying the number of buy or sell trades by $30. Deduct the commissions to calculate your current total portfolio value for the week. Compare this with the value of last week's portfolio and note the difference in dollars. Also indicate whether your portfolio shows an overall gain or loss.

Step 8: List the current value (Friday's closing value) of the four market indexes in Part 2C. Note whether the indexes are moving higher or lower and compare their movement with the week's change in your portfolio's value.

NAME_____ DATE_____

41

CHAPTER 8: UNDERSTANDING STOCK SPLITS

OWNING SHARES DURING A STOCK SPLIT

Top managers never stop watching their corporation's share price and thinking of ways to make the stock more attractive to investors. At times, management may believe that a high share price makes the stock less affordable. To remedy this, the corporation may announce a **stock split**, making each share represent a higher number of shares and reducing the new share price proportionately. (The dividend is usually adjusted by a corresponding amount, as well.)

As an example, when Microsoft (MSFT) announced a 2-for-1 stock split not long ago, the share price on the day before the split was $48.30. On the day the split became effective, each stockholder owned 2 shares for every 1 previously owned, and each share started the trading day at $24.15—half of the pre-split price. Microsoft—like many public corporations—posts information about stock splits on the investor relations section of its Web site (www.microsoft.com).

Some splits give stockholders 3, 4, or even more shares for a single share. Assume that a corporation announces a 4-for-1 split when the share price is $40. After the split, each stockholder owns 4 shares for every 1, and the share price opens at $10—one-quarter of the pre-split price.

A stock split doesn't increase the overall value of the stock held by stockholders. However, it does increase the number of shares outstanding. For example, Microsoft's 2-for-1 stock split raised the number of shares outstanding from about 5 billion to more than 10 billion shares. Not surprisingly, the EPS goes down after a split, because the earnings are spread over more shares. Nonetheless, many investors like owning stocks that are about to split, because they believe the lower share price will attract more investors and demand will drive the price up.

OWNING SHARES DURING A REVERSE STOCK SPLIT

When a corporation wants to increase its share price and decrease the number of shares outstanding, it can use a **reverse stock split**. AT&T (T), for example, once announced a 1-for-5 reverse split that gave each stockholder 1 share for every 5 previously owned. The share price just before the reverse split was $4.97; the share price at the start of trading on the day after was $24.85.

Reverse splits are much less common than the type of split in which stockholders receive multiple shares for each share they already own. A reverse split boosts the EPS, which may make the stock look more attractive to investors. And although it boosts the share price, affordability is not an issue. In fact, the price may be so low before a reverse split that a higher price could very well make the stock seem more appealing to investors.

In some cases, a reverse split helps the corporation remain **listed** for trading on its chosen stock exchange. Major exchanges such as the New York Stock Exchange (NYSE) require corporations to meet certain standards as a condition of being listed. If the corporation's share price, market value, earnings, or other criteria fall below those standards, it risks being **delisted.** Therefore, some corporations use a reverse split to raise the share price and avoid delisting.

ADJUSTING FOR SPLITS AND REVERSE SPLITS

Some corporations, including General Electric (GE) and Microsoft, have announced numerous splits over the years. When you look at the details and charts in their annual reports, however, you don't see any dramatic drops in historic share prices. This is because corporations adjust their per-share prices to account for the effect of stock splits (and reverse splits). Otherwise, investors would be unable to track share prices over months and years.

When you check stock quotes on financial Web sites or in the stock tables, you should see a symbol if a corporation has recently completed a stock split or reverse split. Charts of a corporation's share prices over time usually show adjusted share prices and include a line, arrow, or letter symbol to show the date of a split or reverse split.

Complete these chapter-ending activities to continue your portfolio project.

THINKING CRITICALLY ABOUT INVESTING

1. Would you expect to see more splits or reverse splits during bull markets? During bear markets? Why?

   _____

   _____

   _____

   _____

2. When deciding whether to buy a stock, how much emphasis would you put on an upcoming stock split or reverse split? Why?

   _____

   _____

   _____

   _____

   _____

USING ONLINE TOOLS TO PLAN INVESTMENTS

You can easily find out which stocks recently announced a stock split or reverse stock split using online tools. For example, point your browser to the Yahoo! Finance section at http://finance.yahoo.com. After looking over the main page, follow the link to "stock research." Under the heading "financial calendars," click on "splits calendar" to see which corporations are planning stock splits or reverse splits, when, and other details.

a. Select a corporation that has announced but not yet completed a stock split. When was the split announced and when does it become effective? After the split, how many shares would a stockholder have for single share held before the split?

_____

_____

b. Has any corporation announced a reverse split? If so, how many shares of stock before the split will equal a single share after the split?

_____

_____

c. *Teams:* Get more information about a stock split by Microsoft or another corporation, starting with the Yahoo! Finance site. Then check the investor relations section of that corporation's Web site and search for media releases or news coverage about the split. What kind of split did the corporation plan, and why? What happened to the share price in the period following the split? Do you think shareholders benefited from this split? Explain your answer in a brief report, citing your research sources.

PORTFOLIO ASSIGNMENT FOR CHAPTER 8

1. *Find out about splits or reverse splits.* Use online or library research to determine whether a stock you own has been through a split or reverse split in the past year (or plans some type of split in the near future). Find out how many shares were outstanding before the split and immediately afterward. Also check stock quote tables or the corporation's Web site to see how historical share prices were adjusted for splits in the past. If a stock splits while you own it, adjust your records accordingly.

2. *Research the latest news about each stock you own.* Find out what happened to the corporation and its stock in the past week. Has the corporation recently introduced a new product, launched a new advertising campaign, opened new stores, or changed its marketing in some other way? What is the likely effect on sales, profits, customer relationships, and the share price? If one of your stocks declared or paid dividends during the week, note the amount separately.

3. *Assess stock and market performance.* Look up Friday's last price for each stock and calculate the current value of your positions. Summarize each corporation's situation and discuss how recent developments affected or may affect the share price. Also note the current value (based on Friday's closing value) of the major market indexes.

4. *Decide whether to hold or sell each stock.* Review your research, objective, and risk tolerance as you decide whether to hold or sell each stock. By the end of this project, you <u>must</u> have sold at least one stock and bought another. If you do so on Monday of this week, discuss your decisions and reasoning with a classmate or your team members.

5. *Research at least one more stock for potential purchase.* Research at least one new stock that you would consider purchasing. Be prepared to discuss its recent or planned stock split or reverse split, if any. Follow the rules for purchase if you buy this or another stock.

6. *Calculate commissions and your total portfolio value.* Once you've decided on any trades, add up the number of buy and sell transactions and multiply by $30. Deduct this amount to determine your current total portfolio value for this week. Finally, calculate the difference in your portfolio's value between the current week and the previous week.

After completing these activities, photocopy and complete the Portfolio Project Tracker forms for this week, as in Worksheet #8.

WORKSHEET #8
STOCK SPLITS AND REVERSE SPLITS

Step 1: Review the objective that will guide your portfolio decisions.

Objective?	Amount needed?	When needed?	Long or short term?

Step 2: Note below whether any of your stocks experienced a split or reverse split during the past 12 months (or are planning one very soon). Indicate the type of split and the number of shares outstanding before and after the split. If one of your stocks splits (or already split) during this project, discuss how the share price changed in Part 2A of the Portfolio Project Tracker form for that week.

Stock   Type of split   Number of shares outstanding before and after

_____

_____

_____

_____

Step 3: Copy the portfolio information from Part 1C on last week's Portfolio Project Tracker form to Part 1A on this week's form.

Step 4: Summarize this week's stock research and decisions in Part 2A.

Step 5: If you decide to sell anything based on this week's research or data about splits, use Friday's last share price. Record the trade in Part 1B but wait to record commissions until Step 7. If you are buying any stocks, summarize your research in Part 2A and indicate how the stock(s) can be classified. Document your trades using Friday's last share price in Part 1B (hold commissions for Step 7).

Step 6: Fill out Part 1C to show your positions after this week's trades. Adjust the uninvested cash to reflect your trades. Now add all current holdings to arrive at your total portfolio holdings, and transfer this figure to Part 2B.

Step 7: In Part 2B, calculate this week's commissions by multiplying the number of buy or sell trades by $30. Deduct the commissions to calculate your current total portfolio value for the week. Compare this with the value of last week's portfolio and note the difference in dollars. Also indicate whether your portfolio shows an overall gain or loss.

Step 8: List the current value (Friday's closing value) of the four market indexes in Part 2C. Note whether the indexes are moving higher or lower and compare their movement with the week's change in your portfolio's value.

NAME_____ DATE_____

CHAPTER 9: UNDERSTANDING INITIAL PUBLIC OFFERINGS

INVESTING IN CORPORATIONS THAT GO PUBLIC

When a corporation begins offering shares of its stock to the public for the first time, it is **going public**. The first offering of stock is known as an **initial public offering** or an **IPO**. Corporations use an IPO to raise money for a variety of needs, such as for expansion. For their part, investors buy shares during an IPO because they want to get in on the ground floor as part-owners of a corporation they believe has a bright future.

Here, in simplified form, is how the basic IPO process operates:

- The corporation prepares a **prospectus**, a document to inform potential investors about its financials, management, operations, competition, and market. The prospectus (preliminary at this stage) is filed with the Securities and Exchange Commission. Before you think about buying shares in any IPO, look at the prospectus and research the corporation's situation and its risks.

- After preparing and distributing a more detailed final prospectus, the investment bank *(underwriter)* and the corporation agree on a date for the shares to start trading. No investors will be able to buy any shares before that date.

- Just before the stock starts to trade, a public announcement will be made about the **offering price**, the initial price at which shares will be offered.

- On the first day of trading, the price at which shares of a corporation going public actually begin to trade is the **opening price**.

If buyers are clamoring for shares, the stock's opening price will be higher than the offering price. Sometimes an IPO is so eagerly anticipated that prices rise dramatically during the first day of trading as many investors try to obtain shares. On the other hand, shares can close below the opening price or the offering price on the first day of trading, just as they move up or down on any trading day.

UNDERSTANDING THE RISKS OF IPOS

Stock investments carry no guarantees, and IPOs are no exception. Even the shares of corporations that experience wildly successful IPOs can fall out of favor. The share prices of many Internet-based businesses soared during the IPO boom of the late 1990s, only to plummet within months. Some businesses merged with other corporations, some struggled along, and some had such difficulty that they eventually declared bankruptcy (making their shares worthless).

The bull market of the time had a lot to do with the high number of IPOs. Corporations like going public during bull markets because investors are receptive and shares are more likely to command high offering prices. During a bear market, however, corporations often postpone going public. By waiting until market conditions are more favorable, they hope to set a higher offering price, sell shares quickly, and raise more money.

The average investor has little chance of buying IPO shares at the offering price. Moreover, the opening price can be significantly higher than the offering price when the IPO has received considerable media attention. In fact, one of the risks of getting caught up in a first-day frenzy is that you could wind up overpaying for shares once they begin to trade.

Instead of trying to buy shares on the first day, wait and watch price trends in the weeks and months after the IPO; study the industry; and watch market conditions. Also monitor what analysts and investment publications have to say about the corporation and its stock. After you've done your homework and analyzed the results, you'll have a better picture of the corporation's performance and the price you're realistically willing to pay.

RESEARCHING IPOS

Many financial Web sites, investor newsletters, and business publications report on IPOs. Online, for example, you can get news of upcoming and recently completed IPOs at IPOMonitor.com, Alert-IPO.com, IPOCentral.com, and Edgar Online's IPO Express (www.edgar-online.com/ipoexpress).

In some cases, the Web sites will allow you to compare offering prices and current share prices of IPOs completed months or years ago. You can also read some analysts' commentary and link to other sites for additional research. As with any potential investment, always look beyond analysts' recommendations to learn as much as you can about the corporation and its situation.

For example, established firms such as Krispy Kreme Doughnuts (KKD) and United Parcel Service (UPS) attracted media and investor interest when they went public because of their strong competitive positions and solid reputations. News stories before these IPOs dissected the corporations' financials and strategies and offered multiple perspectives on probable share price trends. After the IPOs, reports followed the corporations' actual performance and tracked the ups and downs of their share prices. Smaller corporations, however, rarely receive this kind of in-depth coverage. That's why you need to dig deeper and consider your risk tolerance level when considering whether to buy IPO shares.

Now complete the following activities to continue your portfolio project.

THINKING CRITICALLY ABOUT INVESTING

1. In general, what are the advantages and disadvantages of buying IPO shares at the opening price?

   _____

   _____

   _____

   _____

2. Why is it important to conduct your own research, going beyond analysts' comments and recommendations when thinking about investing in an IPO?

   _____

   _____

   _____

   _____

USING ONLINE TOOLS TO PLAN INVESTMENTS

One online resource you can use to research corporations going public is the IPO Central section of Hoover's Online. Visit this site at www.ipocentral.com and browse the home page, looking at recently-announced IPOs and other news. Then follow the "Beginner's guide" link and read both the FAQs and the ABCs of IPOs. Now follow the link to the "IPO scoreboard" page.

   a. How many IPOs were priced in the most recent quarter, and in what industries? Is the number increasing or decreasing quarter by quarter?

   _____

   _____

   b. Follow the link to "Best/worst returns." How have recent IPOs fared?

   _____

   _____

   c. *Teams:* Select one of the corporations in the "best/worst" list and research share price trends, industry trends, corporate management and financials, and so on. Also try to locate at least one analyst's comments about this stock. Would you consider buying shares in this corporation today? Summarize your team's thoughts in a brief report.

PORTFOLIO ASSIGNMENT FOR CHAPTER 9

1. *Find out about IPOs.* Using IPO Web sites and corporate information, determine whether any of the stocks you own were issued through an IPO during the past two years. If so, how has the share price changed since the corporation went public? How would your investment have fared if you had bought the stock at its opening price? What are the 52-week high/low share prices, and how do they compare with the share price you paid? If none of your stocks was a recent IPO, select one corporation that is about to go public and research its potential as an investment for your portfolio. Would investing in this IPO fit your risk tolerance and objective?

2. *Research the latest news about each stock you own.* Find out what happened to the corporation and its stock in the past week. Look at how each corporation handles important accounting decisions and manages its information systems. Also consider whether these corporations are effectively using e-commerce to satisfy their customers. If one of your stocks declared or paid dividends during the week, note the amount separately.

3. *Assess stock and market performance.* Look up Friday's last price for each stock and calculate the current value of your positions. Summarize each corporation's situation and discuss how recent developments affected or may affect the share price. Also note the current value (based on Friday's closing value) of the major market indexes.

4. *Decide whether to hold or sell each stock.* Review your research, objective, and risk tolerance as you decide whether to hold or sell each stock. NOTE: Unless your instructor advises otherwise, this is your last opportunity to buy or sell during the project. For peer review, discuss your decisions with a classmate or team members.

5. *Calculate commissions and your total portfolio value.* Once you've decided on any trades, add up the number of buy and sell transactions and multiply by $30. Deduct this amount to determine your current total portfolio value for this week. Finally, calculate the difference in your portfolio's value between the current week and the previous week.

After completing these activities, photocopy and complete the Portfolio Project Tracker forms for this week.

WORKSHEET #9
INITIAL PUBLIC OFFERINGS

Step 1: Review the objective that will guide your portfolio decisions.

Objective?	Amount needed?	When needed?	Long or short term?

Step 2: Note below whether any of the corporations in which you invested had an IPO within the past two years. If so, describe the trend in share prices since the IPO, including the most recent 52-week high/low prices. Discuss the implications in Part 2A of the Portfolio Project Tracker form.

Stock   Date of IPO   Trend in share prices since IPO

_____

_____

_____

Step 3: Copy the portfolio information from Part 1C on last week's Portfolio Project Tracker form to Part 1A on this week's form.

Step 4: Summarize this week's stock research and decisions in Part 2A.

Step 5: If you decide to sell anything based on this week's research or data about splits, use Friday's last share price. Record the trade in Part 1B but wait to record commissions until Step 7. If you are buying any stocks, summarize your research in Part 2A and indicate how the stock(s) can be classified. Document your trades using Friday's last share price in Part 1B (hold commissions for Step 7). Unless your instructor gives you other directions, this is your final opportunity to buy or sell during the project.

Step 6: Fill out Part 1C to show your positions after this week's trades. Adjust the uninvested cash to reflect your trades. Now add all current holdings to arrive at your total portfolio holdings, and transfer this figure to Part 2B.

Step 7: In Part 2B, calculate this week's commissions by multiplying the number of buy or sell trades by $30. Deduct the commissions to calculate your current total portfolio value for the week. Compare this with the value of last week's portfolio and note the difference in dollars. Also indicate whether your portfolio shows an overall gain or loss.

Step 8: List the current value (Friday's closing value) of the four market indexes in Part 2C. Note whether the indexes are moving higher or lower and compare their movement with the week's change in your portfolio's value.

NAME_____ DATE_____

51

CHAPTER 10: UNDERSTANDING MUTUAL FUNDS

CONSIDERING MUTUAL FUND INVESTMENTS

As you learned in Chapter 1, mutual funds pool investors' money to buy a carefully selected portfolio of stocks, bonds, or other securities. Although this project focuses on common stocks, it's important to understand the basics of mutual funds. If you invest through an employer's 401k plan, you may be offered various mutual fund choices. And when you're ready to actually invest your own money, you may want to include mutual funds in your portfolio.

One key advantage to mutual funds is the ability to diversify your holdings. Remember that when you invest in a mutual fund, you become a part-owner of all the securities held by that fund. A second advantage is the ability to tap the expertise of the professionals who are responsible for selecting the securities and making the trading decisions for each mutual fund. You make money through any dividends paid by the fund's securities, any profits from the sale of securities, and any appreciation in the fund's share price.

Despite their convenience, many mutual funds do not perform as well as (or better than) the market's overall performance. Moreover, sales fees and other costs (discussed below) can add to the expense. And investing in mutual funds entails some risk—even more if you choose a fund with a narrow objective or industry focus—so you must keep your objective and risk tolerance in mind. Thus, you can apply many of the skills learned in the course of this project when you examine potential mutual fund investments.

BASICS OF MUTUAL FUNDS

The **net asset value (NAV)** is the price of one share of a mutual fund. The share prices of common stocks change constantly during the trading day, but a mutual fund adjusts its NAV at the end of each trading day, based on the last value of the securities in its portfolio.

Before buying a mutual fund, find out about any minimum investment requirements and any sales charges. If you buy a **no-load fund**, you'll pay no sales charge to buy and sell shares directly through the mutual fund firm (although a commission may apply if you trade through a broker). If you buy a **load fund**, you'll pay a sales fee in one of two ways: either a *front-end fee* (when you buy) or a *back-end fee* (when you sell). Also look at the expense ratio, the percentage of fund assets applied to cover the cost of promotion, management, and other expenses. A lower ratio means lower fees taken out of your returns.

Most funds are **open-end mutual funds**; they can issue more shares at any time in response to investor demand. In contrast, **closed-end mutual funds** start with a specific number of shares and cannot issue additional shares even if investors are eager to buy.

CLASSIFYING MUTUAL FUNDS

The thousands of mutual funds available to investors can be classified in several ways. First, consider the type of securities in the fund's portfolio. Equity funds invest only in stocks; bond funds invest only in bonds; and balanced funds mix both stocks and bonds. Within these categories you can choose from a wide range of highly specific funds to meet your investment needs.

For example, risk-averse investors can buy shares in a fund holding only U.S. Treasury bonds, considered among the safest investments. Investors willing to accept more risk for the potential of higher returns might buy shares in a small-cap equity fund. You can also buy mutual funds that focus on a particular sector, such as the high-tech industry, or a particular area, such as the Pacific Rim.

Second, consider the objective, which is explained in detail in each fund's prospectus. Some of the most common are:

- *Growth funds.* These invest in stocks of corporations that are expanding, seeking long-term growth. Aggressive growth funds buy stocks (including small-cap and mid-cap stocks) that seem poised for more rapid growth and higher share appreciation potential.
- *Income funds.* Some of these invest in stocks with high dividend yields; others invest in bonds with high yields. The objective is to generate current income.
- *Value funds.* These funds seek out bargain stocks that seem to be undervalued. Over time, if the corporations do well, demand for the stock should increase and the share price should rise.
- *Money market funds.* Such funds invest in short-term and extremely liquid securities and strive to keep the NAV at a constant $1. These funds are suited for investors seeking relatively safe, short-term investments with higher returns than traditional bank savings accounts.

A third way of classifying mutual funds is according to management. The mutual funds discussed above are actively managed by professionals who continually research and trade the securities. A special type of mutual fund that is <u>not</u> actively managed is an *index fund,* designed to hold the same securities as a certain market index. You can buy index funds that track the S&P 500, for instance. As the index rises or falls, so does the fund's NAV. An index fund helps you add some diversification to your portfolio. An S&P 500 index fund, for instance, invests only in common stock but it covers 500 U.S. corporations in numerous industries.

A fourth method of classification is according to the fund family offering the mutual fund. Fund families such as T. Rowe Price, Fidelity, and Vanguard offer a wide variety of mutual funds for investors.

RESEARCHING MUTUAL FUNDS

You can check a fund's NAV and other details in mutual fund quotation tables. Exhibit D shows a typical weekly listing.

Exhibit D: Reading a Mutual Fund Quotation

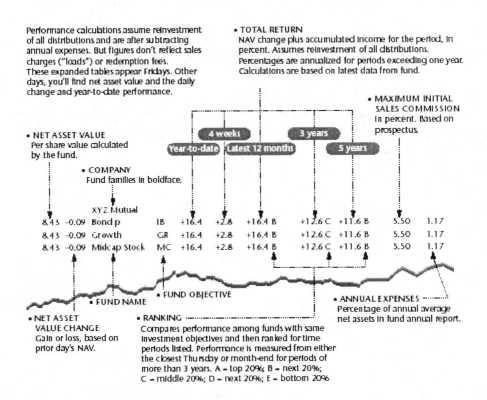

Look up individual mutual funds under the fund family name (XYZ Mutual, in this sample). Quotations show the NAV, change in NAV, returns, load, and annual expenses. (Reminder: the lowest-cost mutual funds are no-load funds with low expense percentages.)

When researching a mutual fund, determine whether its objective and risk fits your objective and risk tolerance. The fund's objective tells you what the manager wants to accomplish with the portfolio of securities. Also look at each fund's returns over various periods and compare the performance with the market's performance during those periods. Then check the ranking of each fund among similar funds. A fund with an "A" ranking has performed better than a fund with the same objective that has an "E" ranking.

Before you invest, __always__ read the prospectus for more detail about a fund's objective, risks, securities, management, and performance. In addition, look up the mutual fund's ratings, rankings, and analysis in financial publications and on Web sites such as Yahoo! Finance. Then make up your own mind, based on your research and your investment situation.

Now complete the following activities to continue your portfolio project.

THINKING CRITICALLY ABOUT INVESTING

1. Why is it important to read a mutual fund's prospectus before buying shares in that fund? What would you look for in a prospectus?

_____

_____

_____

_____

2. Why do you think an investor would buy an index fund rather than an actively managed mutual fund?

_____

_____

_____

_____

USING ONLINE TOOLS TO PLAN INVESTMENTS

Where can you get more on the basics of mutual funds? Visit the Mutual Fund Investor's Center at www.mfea.com. Browse the home page and read one of the current articles posted on the page. Then return to the home page, follow the "fund selector" link, and search using a category that seems to fit your investment objective, such as growth.

    a. Identify one fund family in the search results and look at the listings of two of its funds. How do the two funds differ in terms of classification?

_____

_____

_____

    b. How do these two funds differ in terms of YTD (year-to-date) performance and 5-year performance?

_____

_____

    c. *Teams:* Click on the names of the two individual funds to get more detailed information about the objective, management, minimum investment requirements, and fees of each. Would you consider investing in either of these funds? Summarize your team's thoughts in a brief report.

PORTFOLIO ASSIGNMENT FOR CHAPTER 10

1. *Find out about mutual funds.* Select one actively managed mutual fund and one index fund. Using online or library sources, investigate their objectives, short-term and long-term performance, potential risks, sales loads, and other fees. How would investing in either or both of these mutual funds fit your risk tolerance and objective? How would investing in either or both fit with your portfolio's mix of securities and affect your overall risk? If you had uninvested cash, would you buy shares in either of these funds? Why?

2. *Research the latest news about each stock you own.* Find out what happened to the corporation, its finances, and its stock in the past week. Also investigate what other securities this corporation has issued, and how they are doing. If a stock declared or paid dividends during last week, note the amount separately.

3. *Assess stock and market performance.* Look up Friday's last price for each stock and calculate the current value of your positions. Summarize each corporation's situation and discuss how recent developments affected or may affect the share price. Also note the current value (based on Friday's closing value) of the major market indexes.

4. *Account for any dividends.* If any stocks in your portfolio declared or paid dividends during this project, add up the amount for each stock and note it on this week's worksheet. Even if a dividend was declared but not yet paid, show it on the worksheet. Transfer this information from the worksheet to the line usually used for commissions in Part 2B of the Portfolio Project Tracker. Clearly label it dividend income and *add* it to your portfolio value.

5. *Get ready to evaluate performance.* Gather all the worksheets and Portfolio Project Tracker forms you've completed so far in preparation for evaluating performance (see Chapter 11).

After completing these activities, photocopy and complete the Portfolio Project Tracker forms for this week.

WORKSHEET #10
MUTUAL FUNDS AND MORE

Step 1: Review the objective that will guide your portfolio decisions.

Objective?	Amount needed?	When needed?	Long or short term?

Step 2: Identify two funds that would fit your objective and risk tolerance. Note the names and symbols below, along with their stated objectives. Summarize the advantages and disadvantages of adding these funds to your portfolio.

Mutual Fund/Symbol   Fund Objective   Advantages/Disadvantages

_____

_____

Step 3: Copy the information from Part 1C on last week's Portfolio Project Tracker form to Part 1A on this week's form. Summarize this week's research in Part 2A, but show no decisions.

Step 4: Fill out Part 1C to show your positions using this week's current price. Add current holdings to arrive at your total portfolio holdings; transfer this figure to Part 2B.

Step 5: Calculate all dividends declared or paid for each stock you own (or owned) below, and total all your dividend income for the project.

Stock   # shares   Dividend   Dividend income (# shares x dividend)

_____

_____

_____

_____

_____

_____

Transfer the total dividend income to the line usually used for commissions in Part 2B of the Portfolio Project Tracker. Clearly label it dividend income and *add* it to your portfolio value. (No commissions are deducted this week.)

Step 6: Compare the current total portfolio value with last week's value, note the difference in dollars, and indicate whether you had a gain or loss.

Step 7: List the current value (Friday's closing value) of the four market indexes in Part 2C. Note whether the indexes are moving higher or lower and compare their movement with the week's change in your portfolio's value.

NAME_____ DATE_____

CHAPTER 11: EVALUATING PORTFOLIO PERFORMANCE

CALCULATING RESULTS

How did your portfolio do during the course of this project? This is the time to find out. Be sure you added any dividend income to the current total portfolio value shown in Part 2B of your final Portfolio Project Tracker before you begin. Now look at whether your final portfolio value ended above or below the original $10,000, and by what dollar amount.

Next, analyze the results of your investment decisions in a variety of ways:

- *Week-to-week share-price changes.* Every week, you've noted the purchase and current share price of each stock owned on Part 1A of the Portfolio Project Tracker. Prepare a table (or graph) showing the share price every week from your initial purchase to the final form completed for Chapter 10. For any stocks you sold during this project, prepare a table or graph tracking the share price from purchase to sale.

- *Week-to-week changes in portfolio value.* Using the information in Part 2B of your Portfolio Project Tracker forms, prepare a table or graph showing your total portfolio value for each week, starting with your initial $10,000. As an alternative, your instructor may ask you to show only the weekly gain or loss in portfolio value (from Part 2B) in this table or graph.

- *Return.* How much you make from each investment depends on whether the price increased in value and how much income it generated. To calculate the **return** for your stock—the percentage change in value of a security over a certain period—use this formula:

$$\text{Return} = \frac{(\text{final share price} - \text{purchase share price}) + \text{dividends}}{\text{purchase share price}}$$

Suppose you bought a stock at $33 per share and the share price rose to $43 by the end of the project. If you received $1 per share in dividends from this stock, your return would be:

$$\frac{(\$43 - \$33) + \$1}{\$33} = 33.3\%$$

Calculate the return for each of your stocks, using the share price figures from Part 1C of your final week's Portfolio Project Tracker form. Ideally, you want a good return on each stock, but the overall performance of your portfolio is more important. (Note that you would use more complicated calculations to examine a security's return over several years, calculate the entire portfolio's return, or adjust your return for inflation.)

ACCOUNTING FOR COSTS

Your portfolio's performance, positive or negative, comes at a cost. Every time you buy or sell, you must pay a commission; the more trades you make, the more times you pay your broker. In the long-term, commission costs can be relatively small relative to potential returns; in the short-term, however, frequent trades can erode your portfolio's value. (In reality, you would also look at how taxes affect the money you make, a topic not covered in this supplement.)

Start by adding up the number and dollar amount of commissions you paid during this project, using the information from Part 2B of your weekly Portfolio Project Tracker forms. The next step is to calculate your net profit on each stock. You can do this by deducting the value of the position at purchase (Part 1A of the Portfolio Project Tracker) from the value of the position at the end of the project (or when you sold the stock). Then add the value of any dividends declared or paid for this stock during the project. Finally, deduct the commission you paid to buy this stock, as well as any commission you paid to sell it, to see your net profit.

COMPARING YOUR RESULTS WITH THE MARKET

What happened to the market indexes during the period of this portfolio project? Many investors are unable to meet, let alone exceed, market performance. Thus, whether the value of your portfolio has gone up or down, you should look at your results with an eye toward how the market performed.

Every week, you've noted the current value of four market indexes in Part 2C of the Portfolio Project Tracker. Using this information, prepare a table (or graph) showing the value of each index every week from your initial purchase up through the final form completed for Chapter 10.

Look back and see how weekly changes in your portfolio's value fit with the direction of weekly changes in these indexes. Also look at how the increase or decrease in your final portfolio value compares with the increases or decreases in these market indexes by the end of the project.

REVIEWING YOUR OBJECTIVE AND RISK TOLERANCE

Another way to evaluate your portfolio and its performance is in the context of your investment objective and tolerance for risk. If you're investing for a long-term purpose, is your portfolio making progress toward that objective? If you set a short-term objective, were you able to achieve it?

In addition, examine the composition of your portfolio throughout the project. Were your holdings consistent with your risk tolerance level? Would you now be willing to tolerate more risk for the potential of higher returns? Would you now be willing to trade potentially lower returns for lower risk?

PORTFOLIO ASSIGNMENT FOR CHAPTER 11

1. *Summarize and explain share-price patterns.* Write 1-2 sentences summarizing the share-price pattern of each stock you owned during this project. In addition, based on your weekly research, write 1-2 sentences explaining why you think the share price of each stock changed as it did from your date of purchase until your date of sale (or the end of the project).

2. *Summarize and explain changes in portfolio value.* Write 1-2 sentences summarizing the week-to-week changes in your portfolio's value. Based on your investment decisions and research, write 1-2 sentences explaining the difference between your initial $10,000 and the final portfolio value. Be sure to note the effect of any dividends on your final portfolio value.

3. *Summarize the return for each stock.* Create a table showing the return for each stock in your portfolio. Looking back at your research, explain in a few sentences why you think you got these returns from your stocks.

4. *Look at your costs.* Compare the dollar amount of the commissions you paid with the commissions paid by your classmates (or other teams in your class). Write a brief paragraph discussing these costs in the context of your portfolio's final value and overall performance.

5. *Look at market performance.* Write a paragraph summarizing the pattern and direction of the four major market indexes during this project. In another paragraph, compare market performance with your portfolio's performance.

6. *Think about your objective and risk tolerance.* If your portfolio showed a gain at the end of the project, write a paragraph summarizing your progress toward your investment objective. If your portfolio showed a loss, write a paragraph discussing steps you might take to move toward your objective. Also write a paragraph discussing your attitude toward risk, how it affected your decisions, and what you might do differently when investing in the future.

7. *Gather the latest information about each corporation.* Check one last time to see how each stock fared in the past week. Also research any questions about financial statements or other accounting issues these corporations recently faced and write a brief paragraph summarizing the controversy.

8. *Compare each stock's performance with its industry.* Compare the returns on each stock with the returns of other stocks in its industry.

As your instructor directs: (1) exchange work with a classmate to compare and discuss results; (2) break into small groups to analyze your costs and returns; or (3) compare your returns with the market's performance in class or in teams. *Save your work for use in Chapter 12.*

CHAPTER 12: PRESENTING YOUR PORTFOLIO RESULTS

EXPLAINING YOUR ASSUMPTIONS

The market is closed and all trading completed (for this project, anyway). Now, in this final chapter of *Building Your Personal Stock Portfolio,* you will prepare to present your portfolio results in class or in a written report. The first step is to review and explain the assumptions underlying your investment decisions:

- What objective did you set, and was it a long-term or short-term objective?
- How did your objective affect your choice of stocks and the timing of your trades?
- How did your tolerance for risk affect your choice of stocks and the timing of your trades?

DISCUSSING YOUR DECISIONS

Look back at your investment decisions. What stocks did you buy and why? When and why did you sell one or more stocks? How did each stock choice and trade fit with your objective and risk tolerance? How did you use your weekly research when making decisions about trading?

SUMMARIZING YOUR PORTFOLIO'S PERFORMANCE

Once you've explained your assumptions, you're ready to discuss how your portfolio performed. Using your work from Chapter 11:

- State the return you achieved on each individual stock by the end of the project.
- Compare the final value of your portfolio with the original $10,000 you had to invest.
- Discuss your total trading costs for the project period.
- Discuss your portfolio's performance in the context of your objective and your risk tolerance.
- Compare your portfolio's performance with the market's performance during the project period.
- Compare each stock's performance with the performance of other stocks in its industry.
- Identify any stocks you chose that outperformed the market during the project period and explain why, based on your research.

Remember, building your investments into the highest-value portfolio is not the only measure of achievement in this project. Your portfolio's results may be judged in a number of ways, as shown in Exhibit E.

Exhibit E: Judging Performance in the Portfolio Project

Measure	Purpose
1. Overall portfolio value	To determine how much money the portfolio earned beyond the original investment of $10,000.
2. Direction of portfolio	To determine whether the portfolio's value is moving in the correct direction, if the investment objective was not achieved.
3. Rationale for stock choices	To examine the effect of research, reasoning, objective, and risk tolerance on stock choices.
4. Market performance	To determine whether the portfolio met or exceeded the market's performance.
5. Stock performance	To determine whether a particular stock choice met or exceeded the performance of the market or the industry.

LEARNING FROM YOUR INVESTMENT EXPERIENCE

Buying and selling stocks during this portfolio project gave you the opportunity to research and buy different common stocks without risking real cash. Now it's time to summarize what you learned from this investment experience.

Think about your objective, risk tolerance, research methods and sources, choice of stocks, and trading decisions. What worked well for you—and why? Now think about applying what you learned to the challenge of investing your own money. Discuss any changes you would consider making in the following areas:

- Tolerance for risk
- Research methods or sources used to investigate stocks
- Criteria used to select stock investments
- Timing, frequency, and size of trades
- Measures of portfolio or stock performance

Investing on paper has given you a taste of the decisions and consequences involved in selecting, buying, and selling stocks, without the complications of sophisticated trading instructions, different types of securities, or tax implications. However, this project covered only the most basic principles of investment. Learn more about investing by visiting the Web sites listed in Appendix 1 and by reading books and publications that explain investing in more detail. Remember: The only constant in the market is constant change, so do your homework, get expert advice when needed, and invest wisely. Good luck!

PORTFOLIO ASSIGNMENT FOR CHAPTER 12

1. *Prepare a five-minute presentation summarizing your portfolio project.* Explain your assumptions, discuss your stock choices and trading decisions, and evaluate your portfolio's performance, applying one or more of the measures in Exhibit E. *(Teams: compare results with other teams.)*

2. *Summarize lessons learned.* Write a brief report summarizing what you learned from this portfolio project and what you would do differently if you were going to start investing money today.

3. *Pass along your knowledge.* What single piece of advice would you offer first-time investors? Why is this information important for new investors?

APPENDIX 1:
SELECTED ONLINE RESOURCES FOR INVESTORS

Quotes, News, Screening, and Portfolio Tracking

Money Central (http://moneycentral.msn.com/investor)
CBS Marketwatch.com (www.cbsmarketwatch.com)
Yahoo! Finance (http://finance.yahoo.com)
Quicken (www.quicken.com/investments)
Daily Stocks (www.dailystocks.com)
Bloomberg (www.bloomberg.com)
Morningstar (www.morningstar.com)

Market Information

Dow Jones (www.djindexes.com)
NASDAQ (www.nasdaq.com)
Standard & Poor's (www.standardandpoors.com)
New York Stock Exchange (www.nyse.com)

Corporate Information

Securities & Exchange Commission (www.sec.gov)
Hoovers Online (www.hoovers.com)
IPO Central (www.ipocentral.com)
Best Calls (www.bestcalls.com)

Investor Education

Motley Fool (www.fool.com)
Smart Money (www.smartmoney.com)
Mutual Fund Investor's Center (www.mfea.com)
National Association of Investors Corp. (www.better-investing.org)
Federal Trade Commission information (www.ftc.gov/ftc/consumer.htm)
Investor Guide (www.investorguide.com)
American Association of Individual Investors (www.aaii.com/invbas)

APPENDIX 2:
GLOSSARY

10-K report – report that corporations must file annually with the Securities and Exchange Commission, containing data about finances, operations, risks, and management

10-Q report – report that corporations must file quarterly with the SEC, outlining the same information as the 10-K but in less detail

appreciation – an increase in value, such as if a stock's price goes up

beta - one measure of share price volatility compared with the overall market

blue-chip stocks – large-cap stocks with a long history of profits and dividends

bond – an organization's legal obligation to repay money borrowed by a certain date and to make regular interest payments on that debt

brokers – experts who are licensed to trade securities on behalf of investors, for a fee

bear market – a market in which share prices have been generally on the decline

bull market – a market in which share prices have been generally on the rise

closed-end mutual funds – funds that start with a certain number of shares and cannot issue additional shares

commission – the fee brokers charge investors for trading securities

common stock – a security that gives investors an ownership stake in the issuing corporation and a vote in certain corporate decisions

counter-cyclical stocks – stocks of corporations whose performance runs in the opposite direction from the economy

cyclical stocks – stocks of corporations whose performance is closely tied to the economy's direction

day order – securities order with instructions that apply only on that trading day

defensive stocks – stocks less closely tied to economic cycles and market swings

delist – when a security cannot be traded on a particular exchange because it no longer meets the requirements or is listed on a different exchange

diversify – creating a portfolio with a mix of securities unlikely to be affected in the same way by the same risks

dividends – the amount of a corporation's profits that are distributed to its stockholders

Dow Jones Industrial Average (DJIA) – market index reflecting the stock prices of 30 major U.S. corporations

earnings per share (EPS) – measure of financial performance in which the corporation's net earnings figure is divided by the total number of common stock shares outstanding

face value – the amount of borrowed money that the issuing corporation will return to the investor on the bond's maturity date

futures contracts – agreements requiring the sale or purchase of a commodity at a certain price on a specific future date

gain – the amount by which the value of a security or portfolio exceeds its value at an earlier time (such as at its purchase)

going public – when a corporation begins offering shares of its stock to the public for the first time

growth stocks – stocks with a record of growth that are expected to continue growing and yielding good future investor returns

holding period – time during which an investor owns a security

income stocks – stocks that pay relatively high dividends every quarter

initial public offering (IPO) – the first offering of stock by a corporation that is going public

large-cap stocks – stocks of major corporations that have issued millions of shares and have a high total market value

last – also known as the **closing price,** the share price at which trading ended on a particular day

limit order – securities order requiring the broker to trade a security at a specified price or better

list – when a corporation and its security meet certain criteria and the stock is admitted for trading on a particular exchange

load fund – a mutual fund that charges fees for buying (front-end fee) or selling (back-end fee)

loss – the amount by which the value of a security or portfolio is lower than its value at an earlier time

market order – securities order requiring the broker to buy or sell a security right away, at the best price available at that time

maturity – the date on which the issuing corporation must return a bond's face value to the investor

mid-cap stocks – stocks of corporations with a medium total market value

mutual funds – funds that use a pool of investors' money to buy a select group of stocks, bonds, or other securities

NASDAQ Composite – market index reflecting the stock price of stocks traded over-the-counter through the National Association of Securities Dealers network

net asset value (NAV) – the price of one share of a mutual fund

no-load fund – a mutual fund that charges no sales fee to buy and sell shares

offering price – the price at which a corporation's shares will first be offered in an IPO

open-end mutual funds – funds that can issue more shares at any time in response to investor demand

open order – securities order with limit instructions that stand until the broker executes the trade or the customer cancels the order

opening price – in an IPO, the price at which shares actually begin to trade when the corporation goes public; in a non-IPO setting, the price at which a security begins to trade on a given day

portfolio – the group of securities owned by an investor

position – the number of shares held, share price, and total amount (shares x price) invested in a particular stock

preferred stock – a class of stock that carries a fixed dividend rate but no voting rights

price-earnings (P/E) ratio – an analysis ratio calculated by dividing the corporation's stock price by its earnings per share

prospectus – document filed with the Securities and Exchange Commission by a corporation going public (or a mutual fund firm) to inform potential investors about a security's background, the issuer's finances, and the potential risks

return – the percentage change in an investment's value over a certain period

reverse stock split – when a corporation declares that each share now represents a lower number of shares, raising the share price proportionately and decreasing the number of shares outstanding

risk – in investing, the variability of returns an investor may receive from a security

Russell 2000 – market index covering the stock price of smaller U.S. corporations

securities – investments such as stocks, bonds, and mutual funds

securities analysts – also known as **financial analysts**, specialists who analyze the risks and financial characteristics of stocks and other securities

share buyback plan – also known as a **share repurchase plan** or a **buyback**, a corporation's offer to buy shares back from stockholders at a price that exceeds the market price

shares outstanding – the number of shares a corporation has issued that are owned by investors rather than by the corporation

small-cap stocks – stocks of corporations with a small total market value

Standard & Poor's 500 (S&P 500) – market index reflecting the stock prices of 500 large U.S. corporations

stock dividend – a dividend paid to shareholders in the form of shares of the corporation's stock

stockholders – also known as **shareholders**, individuals and institutions that own shares of the corporation's stock

stock split – when a corporation declares that each share now represents a higher number of shares, decreasing the share price proportionately and increasing the number of shares outstanding

stock symbol – the combination of letters identifying a corporation's stock on the exchange

value stocks – stocks that seem to be priced low relative to their profits and potential

APPENDIX 3:
PORTFOLIO PROJECT TRACKER FORMS

Notes:

1. Photocopy the blank forms for use in completing weekly assignments.

2. Follow the sample forms (which cover a hypothetical portfolio) to see how to enter stock choices and other details in Parts 1 and 2.

SAMPLE PORTFOLIO PROJECT TRACKER – PART 1

PART 1A: YOUR PORTFOLIO BEFORE THIS WEEK'S TRADES

Corporation/symbol	No. shares held	Share price at purchase ($)	Current share price ($)	Value of position at purchase ($)*	Current value of position ($)*	Gain/loss ($)
Apple Computer AAPL	100	19.05	20.10	1,905.00	2,010.00	+ 105.00
Starbucks SBUX	150	23.80	23.55	3,570.00	3,532.50	- 37.50
Home Depot HD	100	32.80	33.05	3,280.00	3,305.00	+ 25.00
						(current value -
						purchase value)
Cash (not invested)	--	--	--	--	1,155.00	--

* formula: # shares x share price

PART 1B: THIS WEEK'S TRADES

Corporation/symbol	No. shares purchased	No. shares sold	Share price at trade ($)	Total amount of trade ($)*
Home Depot HD	30	--	33.05	991.50

PART 1C: YOUR PORTFOLIO AFTER THIS WEEK'S TRADES

Corporation/symbol	No. shares held	Share price at purchase ($)	Current share price ($)	Value of position at purchase ($)*	Current value of position ($)*
Apple Computer AAPL	100	19.05	20.10	1,905.00	2,010.00
Starbucks SBUX	150	23.80	23.55	3,570.00	3,532.50
Home Depot HD	100	32.80	33.05	3,280.00	3,305.00
Home Depot HD	30	33.05	33.05	991.50	991.50
Cash (not invested)	--	--	--	--	163.50

TOTAL 1C PORTFOLIO HOLDINGS: $ 10,002.50 (enter in Part 2B)

NAME_____   DATE_____

SAMPLE PORTFOLIO PROJECT TRACKER – PART 2

PART 2A: RESEARCH AND DECISIONS

Corporation/symbol	News, effect on stock	Buy/hold/sell	Rationale
Apple AAPL	New iPod introduced; online music service gaining popularity; share price rose last week	Hold	Share price likely to increase as computer industry sales improve
Starbucks SBUX	International expansion slowing; competition increasing; share price mixed last week	Hold	Hold until definite share price trends emerge
Home Depot	Home improvement spending up; store-by-store sales up; share price rose last week	Buy 30 more shares	Good potential for higher earnings; P/E seems low for industry

PART 2B: PORTFOLIO PERFORMANCE

Total portfolio holdings (from Part 1C) $10,002.50

Commissions to be deducted (# of trades this week x $30)   - $ 30.00

Current total portfolio value $ 9,972.50

Last week's total portfolio value $ 9,910.00

Change from previous week's total portfolio value (indicate whether **gain** or loss) $ 62.50

PART 2C: MARKET PERFORMANCE

Current value:	S&P 500 984.30	DJIA 9,987.69	NASDAQ 1,742.11	Russell 2000 468.77
Last week's value:	S&P 500 973.72	DJIA 10,055.97	NASDAQ 1,681.45	Russell 2000 464.98
Direction of change:	higher	lower	higher	higher

_____ NAME _____ DATE _____

PORTFOLIO PROJECT TRACKER – PART 1

PART 1A: YOUR PORTFOLIO BEFORE THIS WEEK'S TRADES

Corporation/symbol	No. shares held	Share price at purchase ($)	Current share price ($)	Value of position at purchase ($)	Current value of position ($)	Gain/loss ($)

PART 1B: THIS WEEK'S TRADES

Corporation/symbol	No. shares purchased	No. shares sold	Share price at trade ($)	Total amount of trade ($)

PART 1C: YOUR PORTFOLIO AFTER THIS WEEK'S TRADES

Corporation/symbol	No. shares held	Share price at purchase ($)	Current share price ($)	Value of position at purchase ($)	Current value of position ($)

TOTAL 1C PORTFOLIO HOLDINGS: $ _____ (enter in Part 2B)

NAME _____   DATE _____

PORTFOLIO PROJECT TRACKER – PART 2

PART 2A: RESEARCH AND DECISIONS

Corporation/symbol	News, effect on stock	Buy/hold/sell	Rationale

PART 2B: PORTFOLIO PERFORMANCE

Total portfolio holdings (from Part 1C)	$ _____
Commissions to be deducted (# of trades this week x $30)	$ _____
Current total portfolio value	$ _____
Last week's total portfolio value	$ _____
Change from previous week's total portfolio value (indicate whether gain or loss)	$ _____

PART 2C: MARKET PERFORMANCE

Current value:	S&P 500 _____	DJIA _____	NASDAQ _____	Russell 2000 _____
Last week's value:	S&P 500 _____	DJIA _____	NASDAQ _____	Russell 2000 _____
Direction of change:	_____	_____	_____	_____

NAME _____ DATE _____